INTERVENTIONS

Conor Cunningham and Peter Candler

GENERAL EDITORS

It's not a question of whether one believes in God or not. Rather, it's a question of if, in the absence of God, we can have belief, any belief.

"If you live today," wrote Flannery O'Connor, "you breathe in nihilism." Whether "religious" or "secular," it is "the very gas you breathe." Both within and without the academy, there is an air common to both deconstruction and scientism — both might be described as species of *reductionism.* The dominance of these modes of knowledge in popular and professional discourse is quite incontestable, perhaps no more so where questions of theological import are often subjugated to the margins of intellectual respectability. Yet it is precisely the proponents and defenders of religious belief in an age of nihilism that are often among those most — unwittingly or not — complicit in this very reduction. In these latter cases, one frequently spies an accommodationist impulse, whereby our concepts must be first submitted to a prior philosophical court of appeal in order for them to render any intellectual value. To cite one particularly salient example, debates over the origins, nature, and ends of human life are routinely partitioned off into categories of "evolutionism" and "creationism," often with little nuance. Where attempts to mediate these arguments are to be found, frequently the strategy is that of a kind of accommodation: How can we adapt our belief in creation to an already established evolutionary metaphysic, or, how can we have our evolutionary cake and eat it too? It is sadly the case that, despite the best intentions of such "intellectual ecumenism," the distinctive voice of theology is the first one to succumb to aphony — either from impetuous overuse or from a deliberate silencing.

The books in this unique new series propose no such simple accommodation. They rather seek and perform tactical interventions in such debates in a manner that problematizes the accepted terms of such debates. They propose something altogether more demanding: through a kind of refusal of the disciplinary isolation now standard in modern universities, a genuinely interdisciplinary series of mediations of crucial concepts and key figures in contemporary thought. These volumes will attempt to discuss these topics as they are articulated within their own field, including their historical emergence, and cultural significance, which will provide a way into seemingly abstract discussions. At the same time, they aim to analyze what consequences such thinking may have for theology, both positive and negative, and, in light of these new perspectives, to develop an effective response — one that will better situate students of theology and professional theologians alike within the most vital debates informing Western society, and so increase their understanding of, participation in, and contribution to these.

To a generation brought up on a diet of deconstruction, on the one hand, and scientism, on the other, Interventions offers an alternative that is *otherwise than nihilistic* — doing so by approaching well-worn questions and topics, as well as historical and contemporary figures, from an original and interdisciplinary angle, and so avoid having to steer a course between the aforementioned Scylla and Charybdis.

This series will also seek to navigate not just through these twin dangers, but also through the dangerous "and" that joins them. That is to say, it will attempt to be genuinely interdisciplinary in avoiding the conjunctive approach to such topics that takes as paradigmatic a relationship of "theology and phenomenology" or "religion and science." Instead, the volumes in this series will, in general, attempt to treat such discourses not as discrete disciplines unto themselves, but as moments within a distended theological performance. Above all, they will hopefully contribute to a renewed atmosphere shared by theologians and philosophers (not to mention those in other disciplines) — an air that is not nothing.

CENTRE OF THEOLOGY AND PHILOSOPHY

(www.theologyphilosophycentre.co.uk)

Every doctrine which does not reach the one thing necessary, every separated philosophy, will remain deceived by false appearances. It will be a doctrine, it will not be Philosophy.

Maurice Blondel, 1861-1949

This book series is the product of the work carried out at the Centre of Theology and Philosophy (COTP), at the University of Nottingham.

The COTP is a research-led institution organized at the interstices of theology and philosophy. It is founded on the conviction that these two disciplines cannot be adequately understood or further developed, save with reference to each other. This is true in historical terms, since we cannot comprehend our Western cultural legacy unless we acknowledge the interaction of the Hebraic and Hellenic traditions. It is also true conceptually, since reasoning is not fully separable from faith and hope, or conceptual reflection from revelatory disclosure. The reverse also holds, in either case.

The Centre is concerned with:

- the historical interaction between theology and philosophy.
- the current relation between the two disciplines.
- attempts to overcome the analytic/continental divide in philosophy.
- the question of the status of "metaphysics": Is the term used equivocally? Is it now at an end? Or have twentieth-century attempts to have a postmetaphysical philosophy themselves come to an end?
- the construction of a rich Catholic humanism.

I am very glad to be associated with the endeavours of this extremely important Centre that helps to further work of enormous importance. Among its concerns is the question whether modernity is more an interim than a completion — an interim between a pre-modernity in which the porosity between theology and philosophy was granted, perhaps taken for granted, and a postmodernity where their porosity must be unclogged and enacted anew. Through the work of leading theologians of international stature and philosophers whose writings bear on this porosity, the Centre offers an exciting forum to advance in diverse ways this challenging and entirely needful, and cutting-edge work.

Professor William Desmond, Leuven

BALTHASAR

A (Very) Critical Introduction

Karen Kilby

WILLIAM B. EERDMANS PUBLISHING COMPANY
GRAND RAPIDS, MICHIGAN / CAMBRIDGE, U.K.

Published 2012 by
Wm. B. Eerdmans Publishing Co.
2140 Oak Industrial Drive N.E., Grand Rapids, Michigan 49505 /
P.O. Box 163, Cambridge CB3 9PU U.K.
www.eerdmans.com

Printed in the United States of America

18 17 16 15 14 13 12   7 6 5 4 3 2 1

Library of Congress Cataloging-in-Publication Data

Kilby, Karen.
Balthasar: a (very) critical introduction / Karen Kilby.
p.   cm.
Includes bibliographical references (p.   ).
ISBN 978-0-8028-2738-8 (pbk.: alk. paper)
1. Balthasar, Hans Urs von, 1905-1988.   I. Title.

BX4705.B163K55   2012
230′.2092 — dc23

2012007768

Chapter Five of this work has drawn upon material from within Karen Kilby, "Hans Urs von Balthasar on the Trinity," from Peter C. Phan, *The Cambridge Companion to the Trinity* (2011) © Cambridge University Press 2011, published by Cambridge University Press, and reproduced by permission.

Chapter Six of this work has drawn upon material in Karen Kilby, "Gender in the Theology of Hans Urs von Balthasar," from *Faithful Reading: New Essays in Theology and Philosophy in Honour of Fergus Kerr, OP,* edited by Simon Oliver, Karen Kilby, and Tom O'Loughlin. Published 2012 by T&T Clark International, a Continuum Imprint. Used by kind permission of Continuum International Publishing Group.

For George Lindbeck

Contents

Acknowledgments

Sometimes the link between a volume and the series in which it sits can be rather tenuous, but in this instance the opposite is true. I had never considered writing a book about Hans Urs von Balthasar until a colleague described to me in the coffee room one morning a series of "very critical introductions" he was planning, in which authors would present a major thinker with some seriousness and sympathy, while at the same time developing a substantial critique of this figure's thought. I am grateful therefore to Conor Cunningham and his co-editor Peter Candler for the chance to publish in their series: it has offered me a form through which to develop and articulate a response to Balthasar that had been gestating within me for some time.

I am grateful for the support of the Arts and Humanities Research Council, and the School of Humanities of the University of Nottingham, both of which generously provided research leave enabling the book to be completed.

Audiences at the Universities of Cambridge and Durham, at the Mater Dei Institute in Dublin, at the Institut Catholique de Paris, at St. Johns College, Nottingham, and in my own department have done me the kindness of listening to elements of what is contained here and providing responses that have, or should have, helped to mature the work. I am grateful to them all.

A number of conversations with students, friends, and colleagues have proved useful, and I would like to thank in particular Tina Beattie, Peter Casarella, Mary Gaebler, Henri-Jérome Gagey, Chris Hackett, Nicholas (M.) Healy, Ben Quash, Aaron Riches, Kathryn Tanner, and Anna Williams. Some of these, it should be said, are likely to disagree quite strongly with what follows, but the conversations would not have been so helpful if they had all been with those of a like mind.

For their patience in tolerating my discussions of Balthasar over an extended period I would like to thank my colleagues in the Department of Theology and Religious Studies of the University of Nottingham, and even more so, on the same grounds, my family, especially Andrew, Robert, Sally and John Hunton, and Marianne and Peter Kilby.

Finally, I am grateful for her careful and intelligent editorial work to Katherine Jeffrey.

CHAPTER I

Introduction

A striking feature of twentieth-century Roman Catholic theology is the reversals of fortune which mark the careers of so many of its great figures. Henri de Lubac, S.J., for instance, lived under a cloud for a decade — his own order removed his books from sale, asked him not to teach fellow Jesuits, and even stripped his works from their libraries — but in the early 60s he had a major hand in drafting the documents of the Second Vatican Council, and he finished his life a cardinal. Yves Congar, a Dominican, was forbidden to teach, preach, or write for some time by his superiors, but again emerged as an extraordinarily influential figure in the Second Vatican Council, and he too was made a cardinal before his death. Comparable stories can be told of Marie-Dominique Chenu and to some extent of Karl Rahner.

More spectacular than any of these, however, has been the turnaround in intellectual fortunes of Hans Urs von Balthasar. Like many of the other great theological figures of the century he was ecclesiastically marginalized in the 1950s, but in his case this did not come to an end by 1962; alone among his generation of theologians, he stayed home during the Second Vatican Council. Some time thereafter, however, Balthasar began to be reintegrated, and to gain recognition as a major theological player. As the decades have passed his reputation has only continued to grow. He was said to be the favorite theologian of Pope John Paul II, and is held in high esteem also by Benedict XVI; he is the preferred choice when Anglicans and Protestants look to engage with a Catholic thinker; increasing numbers of Ph.D. dissertations are being written on him;

floods of secondary literature have appeared; and one now frequently hears the judgment that he is *the* great Catholic theologian of the twentieth century.[1]

It is clear that Balthasar is a creative and important thinker from whom there is a great deal to be learned, and that to ignore, marginalize, or dismiss his thought was, and still is, a mistake. The low regard in which he was held in the 50s and 60s (and in the English-speaking world into the 70s at least) was surely not justified. But it is arguable that the pendulum has now swung too far, and that the current tendency to lionize Balthasar, to look to him as some sort of new Church Father, as *the* great figure to emerge in the twentieth century, is also not quite right. Balthasar, for a number of reasons, is no easy figure to absorb or assess, and it is possible that the balance has not yet been found.

This volume is intended as a contribution to the search for such a balance. Balthasar is undoubtedly an important and impressive theologian, and much in his work is original, stimulating, and fruitful. But there is also something fundamentally problematic about his thought, something that should make us wary of looking to him as a general theological model, or as the great voice of tradition in our time. To bring out something of the impressive richness of Balthasar's thought, but also something of what is troubling in it, will be the burden of this volume.

The Difficulty of Finding One's Way around Balthasar

Balthasar, I have mentioned, is not easy to come to terms with. The difficulty, however, is not on the surface; in one sense he writes more accessibly than most modern theologians. He does not import or create large quantities of technical jargon, or produce particularly difficult prose. Any one sentence or paragraph is not especially impenetrable. But to understand where these sentences and paragraphs are going, how they fit

---

1. On the back of English translations of some of his books the claim goes further: "Hans Urs von Balthasar (1905-1988) was one of the greatest theologians of the twentieth century, perhaps of all time." Cf. for example *Heart of the World*, trans. Erasmo S. Leiva (San Francisco: Ignatius, 1979).

together, to get a sense of how his thought is patterned, and what is at its heart, can be unusually difficult. It is easy to feel lost in the fog when reading Balthasar.

A number of things contribute to this difficulty. One is the sheer size of his canon. Not only did Balthasar write a great many works, as we shall see in the next chapter; he also often wrote at great length. *The Glory of the Lord,* for instance, is a seven-volume work of which even the first, introductory volume, the volume to which one might turn in hopes of getting a relatively quick sense of what Balthasar is up to, is 691 pages.[2]

A second source of difficulty is that Balthasar frequently writes in an indirect manner, through collation, exposition, and commentary on the thoughts of others. It is not always easy to keep track of where one is and why one is reading about a particular theologian, philosopher, poet, playwright, or a particular *series* of theologians, philosophers, poets, and playwrights. Balthasar is frequently described, in the words of Henri de Lubac, as "perhaps the most cultivated [man] of his time,"[3] and while the vast range of his learning can surely benefit readers, it can also at times create a fog of impenetrability for those trying to come to grips with his longer works.

Balthasar reports that Adrienne von Speyr, with whom he and his theology were closely connected, would at times rebuke him, and at one point in particular complained about the way in which he wrote:

> When I read what you have written . . . , I sometimes feel you are writing for a totally theoretical person, in other words, for someone who lives only in your mind, a person who has all your presuppositions, who always *à demi* [half] shares your understanding, and this person simply does not exist. So I think it would be good for you to get to know the "normal" man. Somehow you must be brought through him

---

2. *The Glory of the Lord: A Theological Aesthetics,* Volume 1: *Seeing the Form,* trans. Erasmo Leiva-Merikakis (Edinburgh: T&T Clark, 1982). The German original, *Herrlichkeit: Eine Theologische Ästhetik,* Band I: *Schau der Gestalt* (Einsiedeln; Trier: Johannes-Verlag, 1961), was 664 pages.

3. Henri de Lubac, S.J., "A Witness of Christ in the Church: Hans Urs von Balthasar," in David L. Schindler, ed., *Hans Urs von Balthasar: His Life and Work* (San Francisco: Ignatius, 1991), p. 272.

to him. . . . You can't write just for the sake of the subject matter. You have to do it for the reader.[4]

Not all of Balthasar's work fits this description — whether or not in response to the rebuke, Balthasar did in fact write a large number of relatively short pieces that are highly accessible — but von Speyr's comment certainly captures something about the style of his more substantial works. One frequently has the impression that Balthasar is so absorbed by the question under consideration and by his conversation partner (whether that is Maximus or Luther or Buber or Bernanos) that he forgets to think about the kinds of things — signposts, summaries, the setting of context, the explanation of what is at stake — that might help the reader follow his argument. And because, as we shall see in the next chapter, Balthasar was his own publisher, he was never subjected to any external editorial scrutiny or intervention.

A final source of difficulty is again related to one of Balthasar's great strengths, his originality. Balthasar did not divide his work up in conventional ways: one cannot place it in familiar categories, nor watch it unfold according to an expected pattern. What is one to anticipate, for instance, from a work entitled *Theo-drama*? We might know what *sort* of undertaking to expect if someone offers a work of systematics, or, in a Roman Catholic context, an undertaking in fundamental theology. But what genre of project is a "theo-drama"? The reader will not be able to guess in advance, and will not necessarily be enlightened by skimming.[5]

One of the aims of this volume, then, will be to help readers negotiate elements of the fog one encounters in reading Balthasar. The aim is not, however, to provide any kind of exhaustive survey: I will not touch

4. This is a quotation from a letter of von Speyr that Balthasar provides in *Our Task: A Report and a Plan*, trans. John Saward (San Francisco: Ignatius, 1994), p. 94.

5. David Moss and Edward Oakes describe Balthasar as having "more or less single-handedly heaved up a huge mountain range of theology" ("Introduction," *Cambridge Companion to Hans Urs von Balthasar* [Cambridge: Cambridge University Press, 2004], p. 2). They are making the point that he does not stand within a prior school of theology, but this is also a wonderful image for capturing the difficulties for a reader arising from the sheer scope and originality of Balthasar's work.

on all of the themes of Balthasar's work, nor all the thinkers with whom he engaged, nor all the books he wrote. The range of Balthasar's thought is simply too expansive to be helpfully captured in one relatively slim volume. And in any case my goal here is not coverage — not even the limited coverage that might be possible in a slim volume — so much as orientation. Insofar as it affords an introduction, the book will be successful if it can help readers to find their way around in Balthasar's writings, to acquire a sense for some at least of his central concerns, and to come to terms with some of the characteristic patterns, and the characteristic style, of his thought.

The Difficulty of Criticizing Balthasar

Part of coming to terms with Balthasar, I will argue, is coming to terms with what is problematic, what is troubling about him. But this is no easy matter either. For a number of reasons, Balthasar is in fact exceptionally difficult to criticize.

There is first of all the danger that a critic will seem to be rather behind the times: just as children who have once contracted a disease such as chicken pox subsequently have resistance to it, Balthasar's theology has something like an acquired immunity to criticism, or to many forms of it, precisely because it was at one stage so marginalized. If until some point in the 1960s he was largely dismissed, seen as an odd, idiosyncratic character, someone to be ignored because he was not really academically rigorous, and since then he has been, as it were, discovered, then anyone who now might want to object to how idiosyncratic some of his views are, or how little rigor one can find in his writings, is in danger of appearing simply passé. Everybody knows Balthasar is not a standard academic theologian, but we have now, so the thinking runs, gone beyond being so narrow-minded as to be troubled by that. The contemporary critic, in other words, is easily wrong-footed by the very fact that at one stage criticism of him was the norm. Balthasar, who is in fact now so very influential, can nevertheless still be represented as an underdog.

Consider, for instance, the way Balthasar has been presented quite recently in Rodney Howsare's *Balthasar: A Guide for the Perplexed.*[6] This is an excellent introduction to Balthasar — both insightful and readable — and in it Howsare does in fact acknowledge that Balthasar's star has risen in recent years. And yet at regular intervals we find allusions to Balthasar as in one way or another the outsider — suggestions that "Balthasar's theology does not fit easily into the modern university setting" and that there are obstacles to "Balthasar's reception into the academic theological guild" (19); an emphasis on his having been the "*theologian non grata* of both the so-called 'conservative' and 'liberal' wings within the Catholic Church" (144); a characterization of Balthasar's theology as "perplexing to many" because it "does not fit well into either the typically modern approach to theology predominate [sic] in American and European universities, or the typically traditionalist approach which still too often subscribes to neo-scholastic habits of thought" (146). No recent Roman Catholic theologian is more studied, discussed, and generally admired in universities at the moment, and yet he continues to be presented as someone who is usually rejected.

The difficulty in coming to grips critically with Balthasar, however, is not only related to what one might call his reception history. It also has to do with the nature of the work itself. He was, as we have already mentioned, a prolific writer — there are fifteen mostly very substantial volumes in his Trilogy,[7] and beyond this more monographs and collections of essays than is easy to keep track of — and in all this vast output, it is not particularly easy to identify an organizing principle — a point so central that criticism here amounts to a fundamental criticism, a criticism of the whole. How can one, then, *catch hold of* Balthasar well enough to be able to criticize him?

By way of contrast one might think of a figure like Paul Tillich: raise a problem with his method of correlation, or doubts about the value of ex-

---

6. London and New York: T&T Clark, 2009.

7. In English, there are seven volumes which make up *The Glory of the Lord: A Theological Aesthetics;* five volumes in *Theo-Drama: Theological Dramatic Theory;* and three volumes in *Theo-Logic: Theological Logical Theory.* In German, *Herrlichkeit: Eine Theologische Ästhetik, Theodramatik,* and *Theologik* are also published in a total of fifteen *physical* volumes, though they are numbered differently, so that in some cases a single *Band* appears in two physically separate "part-volumes."

istentialism, and one has, it would seem, raised doubts about his theology as a whole. Or Karl Rahner: many have presumed that if one rejects his so-called transcendental method, or else discovers flaws in his early and supposedly foundational philosophical monograph, *Spirit in the World,* then one has found a serious problem with his whole project. Or again Schleiermacher: show why there is something wrong with his notion of the feeling of absolute dependence, and you have perhaps undermined the whole project of his theological maturity. In each case it may be possible to question how fair such approaches to criticism are,[8] but it cannot be denied that such thinkers *seem* at least to give critics a useful target, a relatively easy way to get a handle on their work as a whole. In Balthasar there is no such handle — no central or even apparently central methodological statement, no acknowledged allegiance to a particular philosophical thinker or school, and no one point where it is easy to say: if he is wrong here, something is wrong about the whole business.

A further difficulty arises from the way in which Balthasar argues — or one might say, from the fact that he does not, on the whole, *make* arguments. Balthasar, as I have already mentioned, very often proceeds through extended exposition and survey; somehow in the process, through commentary ranging over several thousand years of thinkers and texts, he presents the reader with the approach he takes to be correct. In an extended sense one might still call this an argument — an implicit argument that this must be the way things are because the vision laid out is compelling, because things hang together and the tradition makes sense if one reads it this way. But there is often no argument offered in any narrower sense of the word.

This *modus operandi* makes critical assessment of Balthasar difficult for two reasons. On the one hand, the range of Balthasar's reading is so vast that it is simply very difficult for a reader or would-be critic to keep up.[9] Someone of a more ordinary level of intellectual culture may be in a

---

8. In the case of Rahner I have written a book arguing precisely that these are *not* good grounds for dismissing him. Cf. Karen Kilby, *Karl Rahner: Theology and Philosophy* (London: Routledge, 2004).

9. The problem, as Kevin Mongrain puts it, of Balthasar's "vertigo inducing level of erudition." Kevin Mongrain, *The Systematic Thought of Hans Urs von Balthasar: An Irenaean Retrieval* (New York: Crossroad, 2002), p. 13.

position to call into question his interpretation of a figure here or there, but Balthasar's range is so huge that questions raised about his faithfulness to any one figure, or even any particular group of figures, can never effectively undermine the vision itself. That Balthasar is not always a perfectly reliable guide to the thought of others is in fact widely recognized: all but the most hagiographic of commentators will grant that he is at least sometimes idiosyncratic as a reader. In general, though, this does not undermine their confidence in him. Even if one finds a commentator suggesting, as Brian Daley does, that on the whole Balthasar's treatment of patristic figures affords better insight into his own thought than into theirs,[10] this makes hardly a dent, for of course Balthasar ranges over not only patristic thinkers, but Greek philosophers and playwrights, Old and New Testament texts, the medievals, mystical writers, a variety of saints, and all kinds of modern philosophy, theology, poetry and drama.

So, on the one hand, there is a kind of elusiveness to Balthasar deriving from the sheer breadth of his learning. And on the other hand there is the fact that, if he can be said to make arguments, they are for the most part not explicit ones. How does one take issue with the argument, find a weakness in the argument, if a vast intellectual landscape is presented but no overt argument actually offered?

Questions of Influence and Suspicions of Heresy

Before attempting an answer to this last question — before saying something, that is, about how I *do* intend to develop a criticism of Balthasar —

10. Balthasar "devoted extraordinary energy and focus to reading those works of the Fathers that attracted him, and he even did primary textual and literary research on some of them. But when all is said and done, he still treated them essentially as sources to support his own theological engagement with modern European culture and thought" (Brian Daley, "Balthasar's Reading of the Church Fathers," in *Cambridge Companion*, p. 189). While Balthasar's treatments of patristic authors are often "brilliant commentaries on these authors within the specialized context of Balthasar's theological project," Daley tells us, "they are usually less than successful in allowing ancient authors to speak clearly to us in their own voices" (p. 202). Balthasar's narrative scheme "leaves the [ancient] authors themselves as largely two-dimensional figures, patches in a modern quilt" (p. 203).

it may be useful to be clear about certain possible lines of criticism which will not be pursued here.

There is, first of all, the question of the relationship of Balthasar's work to the thought and experiences of Adrienne von Speyr. As we shall see in a little more detail in the next chapter, Balthasar worked in close association with von Speyr, took her mystical experiences very seriously, and described their work as two halves of a single whole. How much did she in fact influence him, and if, as he claims, a good deal, is this reliance on the experience of a rather extraordinary mystic with whom he was so close in fact problematic?

This is a critical path I will not be following for a number of reasons. There is, first of all, an issue of complexity here, perhaps even undecidability. Teasing out what influence precisely von Speyr had on him, or indeed in which direction the influence worked, would be no easy matter, given the sheer scope of the writings of each (von Speyr's published output was as enormous as Balthasar's) and the fact that they worked so closely together (not only was Balthasar von Speyr's spiritual director, but von Speyr's writings are all dictations transcribed, edited, and published by Balthasar).

It is of course true that Balthasar insisted that his work and von Speyr's ought not be separated. Nevertheless, he published his volumes of theology under his own name, and for the most part did not, within the texts themselves, appeal to von Speyr's experience to ground the credibility of what he maintained. There are exceptions to this, and the question of the role of von Speyr's work will come into our discussion of Balthasar's treatment of the Trinity, because here he overtly relies on her writings. But on the whole the principle of charitable reading seems to require that we take what he presents at face value, and where he does not present his claims as fundamentally resting on the authority of von Speyr's experience, we should not suppose that they secretly do.[11]

---

11. We shall return to the question of charitable reading in Chapter Seven. For an entirely sympathetic account of the Balthasar-Speyr relationship — one which indeed presents the bond between them as "a specific expression of the living and unswerving bond between God and the human person," see Johann Roten, S.M.'s essay, "The Two Halves of the Moon: Marian Anthropological Dimensions in the Common Mission of Adrienne von Speyr and Hans Urs von Balthasar," in David L. Schindler, ed., *Hans Urs von Balthasar: His Life and Work* (San Francisco: Ignatius, 1991), pp. 65-86 (quotation from p. 85). For a dis-

One could also ask about influence on a broader scale. Is there, for example, a major debt to Heidegger,[12] and might this problematically shape Balthasar's thought in some way? Is there something distinctly Hegelian in his thinking, even though he is overtly critical of Hegel?[13] Or is his theology more generally, perhaps, in the grip of German romanticism?[14]

Such questions of influence will not take center stage in this treatment of Balthasar. The principal focus will be, again, on Balthasar as one actually encounters him in his works, rather than on the rather complex issue of what may or may not lie behind his thought. This is not to suggest that issues of influence are uninteresting or un-illuminating, but they are often highly contested, and to attempt a critique of Balthasar by way of the tracing of influence would not be an especially helpful approach in a volume that is also intended as an introduction, unless the introduction were aimed, rather arbitrarily, only at those who already have an expert's grasp on Hegel, Heidegger, and the whole idealist and romantic German tradition. For many readers, in other words, an argument framed in terms of the antecedents of Balthasar's thought would function as a distraction from rather than a shortcut to the understanding of Balthasar himself. In any case, of course, if there is a problem in relation to the hold that some figure or other — whether Hegel or Heidegger or von Speyr — has on Balthasar, such a problem should also manifest itself as a weakness in the fabric of Balthasar's *own* thought.[15]

---

tinctly more critical consideration of this relationship, cf. Tina Beattie's *New Catholic Feminism: Theology and Theory* (London and New York: Routledge, 2006), especially Chapter 8, "Desire, Death, and the Female Body," pp. 149-62.

12. Fergus Kerr emphasizes the importance of Heidegger for Balthasar's metaphysics in "Balthasar and Metaphysics," in *The Cambridge Companion to Hans Urs von Balthasar,* pp. 224-39. Though Rahner attended Heidegger's classes and Balthasar did not, "Balthasar is far more Heideggerian than Rahner ever was" (p. 225).

13. Cf. Ben Quash's *Theology and the Drama of History* (Cambridge: Cambridge University Press, 2005) for a careful exploration of this issue.

14. See, for example, Nicholas Boyle, "'Art,' Literature, and Theology: Learning from Germany," in Robert E. Sullivan, ed., *Higher Learning and Catholic Traditions* (Notre Dame: University of Notre Dame Press, 2001).

15. Probably the most disturbing question of influence on Balthasar's thought thus far raised is the question of the impact on at least his early writings of the ideology of National Socialism. In a fascinating article, and one that looks to be the beginning of an important discussion, Paul Silas Peterson examines Balthasar's early *Apokalypse der deutschen Seele*

Balthasar is often described as "idiosyncratic" as regards some at least of his theological positions, and it is possible to question whether, in this idiosyncrasy, he remains within the bounds of orthodoxy. This is a line or argument that has recently been very vigorously pursued by Alyssa Lyra Pitstick in relation to Balthasar's treatment of Christ's descent into hell.[16] Pitstick's is a fascinating book, and in its own way a real tour de force. Both in its framework of argument,[17] however, and its rhetoric,[18] the book is suggestive of precisely the kind of neo-scholasticism that Balthasar, as we shall see in the next chapter, emphatically rejected. In any case, the question of whether Balthasar was heretical will not form the basis for this study. That Balthasar, while he might be seen as a conservative, is at many points certainly not traditional, will I think emerge quite clearly and will not be in need of a great deal of argument. And while it would be a mistake simply to assume that where his thought is unusual it must also contain deep new spiritual insights, or

---

and points to a range of elements in the rhetoric, the choice of themes, the historical narrative and the choice of authors that involved Balthasar's "draw[ing] Christianity into a narrative which is compatible with the new Germanic myths." Peterson also highlights strikingly anti-Semitic passages in this work. Paul Silas Peterson, "Anti-Modernism and Anti-Semitism in Hans Urs von Balthasar's *Apokalypse der deutschen Seele*," in *Neue Zeitschrift für Systematische Theologie und Religionsphilosophie* 52/3 (2010): 302-18.

16. Alyssa Lyra Pitstick, *Light in Darkness: Hans Urs von Balthasar and the Catholic Doctrine of Christ's Descent into Hell* (Grand Rapids: Eerdmans, 2007).

17. Pitstick first sets out the "traditional Catholic doctrine of descent" through an examination of "multiple objective repositories of the Faith" (p. 342), then examines Balthasar's theology of Christ with a principal goal of demonstrating the departure of the latter from the former. Her conclusion is that "Balthasar's *descensus* theology fails to adhere to the only sure guide and standard of truth in this matter; more, it contradicts it. For this reason alone — setting aside all the reasons of theological argumentation seen throughout this work — his *descensus* theology cannot be true, nor is it an expression of the Catholic Faith" (p. 346).

18. For instance, at the beginning of the book Pitstick formulates her aim as follows: "to consider whether a triumphal descent by Christ or a descent to suffering is the true expression of the Catholic Faith" (p. 2) and towards the end, after noting the obscurity of Scripture on the question of Christ's descent, Pitstick writes: "necessarily either we rely upon Tradition as an infallible guide to revealed truth and upon the ability of reason enlightened by faith to identify that Tradition under the magisterial guidance of the Church's hierarchy — or we *de facto* reject such Tradition in whole or in part" (p. 346). There is a distinctive *style* of theological writing here, and it is the style of neo-scholasticism.

herald a development in doctrine, it might also be wrong to rule out these possibilities in principle.[19]

The Jigsaw

Jacques Servais begins an essay entitled "Balthasar as Interpreter of the Catholic Tradition" with a brief but intriguing story:

> Balthasar had a chalet in the village of Rigi, perched high in the Swiss Alps where he would spend vacations working, often with de Lubac. One evening, I and another — then young — Jesuit were there with them and, knowing Balthasar to be an aficionado of handmade puzzles, we set out to complete a particularly difficult one, with plenty of blue sky and no two pieces quite the same. As the evening drew on, so did our perplexity: we were puzzled by the heavens, divided out as they were into many tiny pieces on the table before us. Balthasar watched from a distance, tempted to help but holding back, while de Lubac began pacing beside us: perhaps a bit agitated because we were delaying the daily evening get-together. Finally, Balthasar walked up and joined us, picking up a piece, and putting it into place, then the next, and the next, until the whole puzzle was finished, and in less than ten minutes. We, quite frankly, would probably have been there for ten hours.[20]

19. This is not to say that it could never be relevant to ask whether a thinker is orthodox or heterodox. Clearly not everything in the Catholic tradition is up for grabs, and not just any kind of proposal might count, or even be considered as a possible candidate to count, as development of doctrine. Whatever it *might* be possible to say about Balthasar on this score, however, fundamentally I do not think that the categories of heresy and orthodoxy provide the most helpful way to approach him — the most helpful way, that is, either to gain a sense of what he is up to, or to articulate what is most deeply troubling about his work. Nevertheless, there is something very impressive about Pitstick's book; if initially it may appear both narrow in aim (to establish that Balthasar's position is not orthodox) and narrow in focus (on the meaning of Christ's descent into hell), it turns out to engage with Balthasar's thought across a broad spectrum, and in an analytically impressive manner.

20. "Balthasar as Interpreter of the Catholic Tradition," in David L. Schindler, ed., *Love Alone Is Credible: Hans Urs von Balthasar as Interpreter of the Catholic Tradition* (Eerdmans: Grand Rapids, 2008), p. 191. I am grateful to Chris Hackett for directing my attention to this essay.

Servais presents this story as an example, and perhaps also as a symbol, of Balthasar's "Johannine vision of the whole." This is not an unreasonable place to begin an essay, for the notion of the whole, and of the *vision* of the whole, and of the relation of the part to the whole, are all very important themes for Balthasar. And if we take the story itself to suggest that Balthasar operated with a speed and confidence very different from those around him, then anyone who considers the sheer quantity of writing and editorial work he did will be hesitant to object.

And yet if we think of this little story in the context in which Servais sets it — in the context, that is, of an exploration of Balthasar *as interpreter of the Catholic tradition* — it might also give pause. Is Balthasar, with the Catholic tradition as with the jigsaw puzzle, one who stands above and effortlessly assembles, putting each thing in its place until the whole is completed? There is a sense of mastery here, of effortless authority and superiority, of privileged access, even, which might be unsettling.

What I want to propose is that, although this was certainly not Servais's intention, the image serves to illustrate a troubling feature of Balthasar's theology. Balthasar frequently writes as though from a position above his materials — above tradition, above Scripture, above history — and also, indeed, above his readers. He frequently seems to presume, to put the point in its sharpest and most polemical form, a God's eye view.[21]

This proposal is not intended, it is important to be clear, as a criticism of an *articulated* method. Balthasar does not anywhere explicitly lay claim to a God's eye view, to a position above all tradition, Scripture,

---

21. This is not intended to be a personal criticism of Balthasar. What is at stake is not whether, as an individual, he was presumptuous or humble, nor what his private opinion of his abilities may have been. Technically perhaps, one should say that what is at issue is the location of the implied author of Balthasar's works, and the nature of the authorial voice which comes through in them.

At one point in his *Theology and the Drama of History*, specifically in connection with knowing what is and is not significant in history, Ben Quash also writes of Balthasar's "presumption to have a God's eye view" (p. 197). In general Quash's study has a different shape from this one — his is an examination of Balthasar in relation specifically to Hegel and Barth, and with a particular focus on the notion of theodramatics — but there are nevertheless, in my judgment at least, distinct affinities between the critique I will develop and the one that emerges from his work.

and so on. And indeed it is not difficult to find passages in which he specifically acknowledges the limited nature of our knowing, the need for epistemic humility, the inescapability of mystery. What I will be trying to show is that Balthasar is in fact caught in a significant performative contradiction: the way his theology is done presumes something which the content of the theology rules out.

This is, it must be acknowledged, a rather strong criticism. I am not suggesting merely that *at times* Balthasar oversteps a boundary, that every now and then he goes beyond the limits of what a theologian can properly say, that every now and then he seems to know too much. I am suggesting rather that the presumption of a position above Scripture, tradition, and history, and also above his readers, permeates a great deal of his work. This is more to be viewed as the characteristic mode of his theology, I will try to show, than as an occasional excess.

The Shape of This Volume

The critical argument of this book cannot, for reasons suggested above, proceed through an exhaustive survey of all that Balthasar has written. But how then can one hope to say something of a broad nature about his thought? One way will be through an analysis of certain images and patterns that structure and shape his thought. After an initial chapter considering the contexts out of which and into which Balthasar wrote, then, Chapters Three and Four will focus on four key images, and on exploring the implications of Balthasar's use of these for his own position in relation to his materials and his readers. The next two chapters will then develop case studies, looking at Balthasar's treatment of the doctrine of the Trinity on the one hand and the role of gender in his thought on the other. In Chapter Seven, after briefly drawing the strands of the argument together, I will consider a number of objections that might be made to the argument that has been laid out. The argument as a whole will be cumulative. At each stage, perhaps, it will be possible to wonder whether there might not be some other way of reading Balthasar, some way to shield him from criticism; or it will be possible to wonder, at least, whether these critical points might be taken as relatively minor in relation to the heart of his theology. If the argument is successful, it will be because, cumulatively, it becomes clear that over-reaching is not an occasional or peripheral feature of Balthasar's thought, but something right at its core.

One might suppose that a book intended to be both introductory and critical ought to proceed in that order, beginning with an expository section and only as a second step moving on to critique. It will be clear from the brief outline just given, however, that that is not the approach to be followed here. Exposition and critique are in fact interwoven in nearly every chapter that follows. This might seem, but will not in fact be, I hope, a formula for unfairness to Balthasar. It should be clear in nearly all the chapters that follow that I think there is much to admire, much to appreciate, and much to appropriate, in what Balthasar does. But it is not especially helpful — and for the kind of argument I want to develop, not even possible — to postpone critique until after one has finished explaining and appreciating, to insist that appreciation and critique must be kept sharply separated from one another. The best approach to Balthasar, I believe, is always to approach him with *both* openness (for he may well overturn one's assumptions in a way that is both surprising and edifying) and a certain wariness.

CHAPTER 2

The Contexts of Balthasar

One has a right to expect, in any introduction to a major thinker, at least some description of his or her context. In this case, however, what is at stake is more than mere background: the pattern of Hans Urs von Balthasar's education, the course of his life, and the conditions in which he worked were in fact unusual among twentieth-century Catholic theologians, and they are contributing factors, I will suggest, to both the best and the worst features of his writings.

Education

Balthasar was born into "an old patrician family"[1] in Lucerne, in the German-speaking part of Switzerland, in 1905 — a year later than Karl Rahner, nine years after Henri de Lubac, and when Karl Barth, another Swiss German, was already nineteen. He did his school leaving exam a year ahead of schedule, and then took up *Germanistik*[2] at the universities of Zurich, Berlin, and Vienna. This is worth noting: Balthasar did not,

---

1. These are the words of Peter Henrici, S.J., the Blondelian philosopher who was also his cousin. Henrici has written a very helpful biographical piece, "Hans Urs von Balthasar: A Sketch of His Life," which can be found in David L. Schindler, ed., *Hans Urs von Balthasar: His Life and Work* (San Francisco: Ignatius, 1991), pp. 7-43. The quotation is from p. 8.

2. *Germanistik* is the study of German literature, but in a somewhat broader sense than we are used to using. It might equally be described as the study of German literature and philosophy.

like many of his contemporaries (e.g., Rahner or de Lubac) enter the Jesuits straight out of secondary school, and his studies did not begin with philosophy and theology.

In 1928, at the age of twenty-three, Balthasar completed his doctorate in *Germanistik*. That same year, having experienced a dramatic call from God — under a particular tree in the Black Forest near Basel he was "struck as if by lightning"[3] — he joined the Jesuits (officially, "the Society of Jesus," a religious order founded by St. Ignatius of Loyola in 1540, and known for its strong intellectual orientation). The Jesuits did not have official recognition in Switzerland, and so Balthasar's training was elsewhere: a two-year novitiate in Feldkirch in Austria (where he had also completed his final two years of secondary school), two years of philosophy in Pullach, near Munich in Germany, and then four years of theology at Fourvière, near Lyons in France, after the third of which he was ordained a priest.

To understand the way philosophy and theology were taught in the 1930s at Pullach and Fourvière, or indeed anywhere in the Catholic world, it is necessary to look back to certain developments in the previous century. Among the various schools of Catholic thought competing with each other in the middle of the nineteenth century, one advocated a return to the thought of Thomas Aquinas (1225-1274), as seen through the lens of early modern commentators. In 1879, in the encyclical *Aeterni Patris*, Pope Leo XIII gave official approval to this nineteenth-century revival of a seventeenth-century interpretation of St. Thomas. The formal philosophical and theological education of priests and theologians of Balthasar's generation, then, took place entirely within the system of what came to be known as neo-scholasticism. And neo-scholasticism was indeed a *system*, a complete, self-enclosed whole, encompassing both philosophy and theology. As a thought world, it was tidy, orderly, and in no need of anything outside itself. Certain questions were open, upon which there could be disagreement and debate, but these were limited and well-defined, contained in a larger structure where everything important was essentially

---

3. *Pourquoi je me suis fait prêtre* (Tournai: Editions Centre Diocésain de Documentation, 1961), p. 21, cited in Edward T. Oakes, S.J., *Pattern of Redemption: The Theology of Hans Urs von Balthasar* (New York: Continuum, 2002), p. 2, note 2.

known and already in its proper place. It was a dry, rationalist approach to philosophy and theology, more profoundly a reaction against modern culture than a real return to the thought of Thomas.

Balthasar did not take to this at all. Famously, he wrote of his time of study in the Jesuits as "a grim struggle with the dreariness of theology, with what men had made out of the glory of revelation. I could not endure this presentation of the Word of God! I could have lashed out with the fury of a Samson."[4]

Balthasar's response to the deficiencies of his official education was essentially to occupy himself with other things, and to avail himself of educational possibilities beyond the official curriculum. During his philosophical training, he was in contact with Erich Przywara, a prolific and influential Jesuit philosopher and intellectual who lived in Munich and edited *Stimmen der Zeit*. Balthasar was later to spend a couple of years living with Przywara and working on *Stimmen der Zeit* with him; later still he would defend Przywara's understanding of *analogia entis*, the analogy of being, against Karl Barth, who notoriously took it to be an "invention of the anti-Christ." He took advantage of his time in France by reading French literary figures, several of whom he was eventually to translate into German: Claudel, Peguy, Bernanos, Mauriac. He substantially revised and expanded his doctoral thesis, which was eventually published in three volumes as *Apokalypse der deutschen Seele*.[5] He also

4. From Balthasar's Introduction to von Speyr's *Erde und Himmel: Ein Tagebuch,* Zweiter Teil: *Die Zeit der großen Diktate* (Einsiedeln: Johannes Verlag, 1975), cited in *Pattern of Redemption*, p. 2. It is clear that Balthasar continued to have a low opinion of this mode of doing theology and philosophy throughout his life, but in the reference here to the "fury of a Samson" there seems also to be a certain element of self-criticism. Balthasar goes on to write that "it was like this because, despite my sense of vocation, I wanted to carry out my own plans, and was living in a state of unbounded indignation."

5. The first volume appeared in 1937, and the second and third in 1939. We will not have occasion in what follows to return to this early work, which Balthasar subsequently wrote about with a certain sense of distance, but certainly never repudiated. It is worth noting in passing, however, three things: first, that it was already, like much that Balthasar was later to do, an enormously ambitious project, claiming to diagnose the state of the "German soul" through a long tracing of literary history; second, that we find here already a strong polemic against modernity; and third, as Paul Silas Peterson has recently shown, that some of these three volumes at least are marked by a definite and very troubling anti-Semitism, and more broadly, or so Peterson has argued, have distinct resonances with the

read widely in the writings of the Church Fathers, which eventually led to his volumes on Origen, Gregory of Nyssa, and Maximus the Confessor.[6]

De Lubac

In his reading of the Fathers Bathasar was guided by Henri de Lubac, S.J., who, though not formally one of his teachers, was at Fourvières during his time. De Lubac's own theological education was disrupted by the First World War, and he was mainly self-taught.[7] He and Balthasar were to remain friends, and theologically close, throughout Balthasar's life (de Lubac, though the older of the two, outlived Balthasar).

De Lubac has to be counted, on almost any reckoning, among the handful of leading Catholic theologians of the twentieth century. He wrote a number of seminal books, including *Catholicism,* a study, as its French subtitle indicates, of the social aspects of dogma, and *Corpus Mysticum: The Eucharist and the Church in the Middle Ages,* a volume which set in motion twentieth-century Catholic interest in "Eucharistic" or "communion" ecclesiology. But he is probably best known for his *Surnaturel,* a book which appeared in 1946 and provoked a massive controversy. The vision of nature and grace, and therefore also of faith and reason, and philosophy and theology, towards which de Lubac's book pointed was tremendously important for Balthasar, and it is worth saying at least a little about it at this stage.

The issue at the heart of *Surnaturel,* and at the heart of the controversy it provoked, can from one perspective seem extraordinarily narrow and technical. De Lubac maintained, and his opponents denied, that

---

"new Germanic myths" of the time. Cf. Paul Silas Peterson, "Anti-Modernism and Anti-Semitism in Hans Urs von Balthasar's *Apokalypse der deutschen Seele,*" in *Neue Zeitschrift für Systematische Theologie und Religionsphilosophie* 52.3 (2010): 302-18.

6. These early books have turned out to be important ones. Balthasar's study of Maximus, in particular, triggered a significant revival of interest in this seventh-century figure.

7. Cf. Fergus Kerr's chapter on de Lubac in *Twentieth-Century Catholic Theologians* (Oxford: Blackwell, 2007), particularly pp. 67-69. This is more generally a helpful treatment of de Lubac, as is also John Milbank's *The Suspended Middle: Henri de Lubac and the Debate Concerning the Supernatural* (Grand Rapids: Eerdmans, 2005).

there is "natural desire for the supernatural." Or more precisely, de Lubac maintained that belief in the existence of a "natural desire for the supernatural" was traditional, that this belief had been held by many thinkers before Thomas Aquinas, and that it was held by Aquinas himself. His opponents, the neo-scholastics, who considered themselves to be following St. Thomas, denied that there could be a natural desire for the supernatural, or that Thomas maintained that there was such a thing.

The distinction between the "natural" and the "supernatural" here is a distinction between what we are as created, according to the "nature" which God has given, and what we may become when elevated *beyond* our nature, through a further gift of grace. What the neo-scholastics proposed — and what de Lubac thought both wrong and out of step with the earlier tradition — was that human nature had a kind of completeness, a self-sufficiency, and that it was thus in principle (leaving aside questions of sin for the moment) capable of a "natural beatitude," a natural happiness. In his insistence on the "natural desire for the supernatural" de Lubac was rejecting this view: we are made from the start so that we *cannot* be fulfilled unless taken beyond ourselves, elevated above our nature. Nature is in a sense always already oriented towards and longing for grace, always incomplete if left to itself.

On the view propounded by de Lubac, and very much absorbed and made his own by Balthasar, while the distinction between nature and grace remains necessary, nature and grace do not form tidily distinct spheres. And this has, it turns out, very wide implications — implications about how one understands the relation of faith and reason, for instance, or the relation of philosophy and theology. Reason cannot be a kind of neutral power sharply distinguished from faith, but will be seen as by its very nature wanting to reach beyond itself, searching for something it cannot itself provide. Philosophy, similarly, will not be considered intrinsically indifferent to or neutral towards theological matters, but as driven by its own inner impulses to seek and to point to, or somehow open itself up to, what lies beyond its boundaries.[8] More broadly

---

8. The corollary of this is that if one comes across a kind of philosophy which seems to show no such impulse, one will have to consider it to be somehow truncated, lost, out of touch with its own most proper roots — not, in short, a true philosophy.

still, the world as a whole will not fundamentally be conceived as either hostile to or even neutral towards the Church, but as the sphere in which there is necessarily a seeking for what is not yet found, an inchoate, inarticulate desire for the faith, the beginnings and struggles towards something which cannot be found within the world's own resources.

One further point about de Lubac that needs mentioning here has to do with method. De Lubac's theological arguments were always indirect — he operated in a historical mode, never presenting his alternative to the prevailing consensus in his own voice, but doing so instead by the way he laid the tradition before his readers — typically moving among large numbers of thinkers and mustering masses of quotations. His method of fighting against what he took to be the deformations of neo-scholasticism, in other words, was to bring to the fore an enormous weight and breadth of past voices, weaving together the tradition before his readers' eyes in such a way that the position of his opponents would come to seem untenable. So in de Lubac one finds both indirection — argument through extended exposition of the views of others — and an effort to reconfigure contemporary thinking through exposure to a vast array of earlier sources. Both qualities are relevant for an understanding of Balthasar's work.

Useful as it is to understand Balthasar in connection with de Lubac, it is equally helpful to see *both* as in fact part of a broader phenomenon, a deeply impressive generation of Catholic theologians united not so much by a common education as by a common reaction against this system in which they were, or were supposed to have been, educated. The imposition of neo-scholastic uniformity seems to have given birth to a tremendous collective impulse both to go *back* — back to the real Aquinas as opposed to the one presented in the system, and back also beyond Thomas to the richness and beauty of patristic thought — and to go *out,* out beyond the narrow confines of thinking within the Church to an engagement with something much broader and more alive in contemporary thought. In Balthasar's case we have seen both the backward and the outward movements already in evidence during the years of his official theological formation — back to the Church Fathers, out into the realm of French literature.[9]

9. For a very helpful guide to the whole generation, see Gabriel Flynn and Paul D.

If the reaction against neo-scholasticism is a unifying theme among the major Roman Catholic theologians of the twentieth century, the way in which this reaction took shape was nevertheless varied. Karl Rahner, for instance, had entered the Jesuits at eighteen, straight from secondary school, and the neo-scholastic formation seems to have made a significant impression on him; much of his theology can be interpreted as a dismantling of neo-scholasticism *from within,* constantly showing, for instance, that there were more profound difficulties, more open questions, and more room for different approaches than was usually supposed. De Lubac, as we have seen, fought against neo-scholasticism not so much by unpicking it from within as by mustering the evidence of tradition against it at decisive points, as in *Surnaturel.* In Balthasar one finds neither the careful internal criticism of neo-scholastic assumptions of a Rahner, nor, though he was close to de Lubac, the concerted attack from without of the latter. At first sight he seems simply to have left neo-scholasticism to one side, refused to engage with it at all, and proceeded to do theology in a radically different way. We are told that he put wax in his ears during lectures in order to work his way through the whole of Augustine's corpus for the sake of producing an anthology,[10] and it is easy to think of this wax in the ears as symbolizing Balthasar's whole relationship to neo-scholasticism. It would probably be wrong, however, to assume that he remained entirely unaffected by it. One finds scathing references throughout Balthasar's writings to those who would try to make of revelation a "system," which seem to suggest that the specter of neo-scholasticism was never far from his mind. It would not be unreasonable to read a good deal of his work as a reaction against neo-scholasticism, precisely insofar as it aims to show how theology and philosophy can be done in a radically different manner.[11]

Murray, eds., *Ressourcement: A Movement for Renewal in Twentieth-Century Catholic Theology* (Oxford: Oxford University Press, 2012).

10. "Hans Urs von Balthasar: His Cultural and Theological Education," in Bede McGregor, O.P., and Thomas Norris, eds., *The Beauty of Christ* (Edinburgh: T&T Clark, 1994), p. 12.

11. Thus Kevin Mongrain, for instance, can write of "the adversarial agenda of [Balthasar's] post-seminary intellectual career." See his *The Systematic Thought of Hans Urs von Balthasar: An Irenaean Retrieval* (New York: Crossroad, 2002), p. 2.

Upon the completion of his studies, Balthasar worked for a time for the German Jesuit periodical *Stimmen der Zeit* ("Voices of the Times") which Przywara edited. He was then offered a choice: to go to the Gregorian University in Rome to become a theology professor, or to return to Switzerland to take up a position as university chaplain in Basel. Balthasar chose the latter.

The choice of Basel over Rome, a chaplaincy rather than a career at one of the leading universities in the Catholic world, is frequently taken as an indication of Balthasar's strong pastoral orientation, and to some degree it is. But to fully understand the significance of his decision, the options he faced need to be considered a little more carefully. On the one hand, what he turned down was not just a prestigious academic position, but more particularly an academic position in the context of the dominant neo-scholasticism: given his utter distaste for neo-scholasticism, it is not entirely surprising that he would be reluctant to take up such a post.[12] And, on the other hand, what he chose needs to be seen not just as pastoral work, nor even just pastoral work with young intellectuals. Switzerland at the time was hospitable neither to Jesuits nor to Catholic theology; there were no university departments in which one could teach as a Catholic theologian, and no Jesuit seminaries. In taking up the role of university chaplain, then, Balthasar was placing himself in a rare position from which he could as a Catholic engage with the high culture and intellectual life of his native land. His choice, then, to go to Basel, was as much a choice for Switzerland over Rome, and for the breadth and freedom of a broad cultural engagement over the narrow confines of an institution dominated by neo-scholasticism, as it was a choice of the pastoral over the academic.[13]

---

12. The particular role that Balthasar would have had at the Gregorian was, along with three others, to establish an institute for ecumenical theology. Clearly he would have been engaging in something of a new venture, but the fundamental context would still have been that of neo-scholasticism.

13. In the early 1940s student chaplaincy meant, above all, "cultural work." See Henrici, "Sketch of His Life."

Karl Barth

Two people in Basel turned out to be extremely important for Balthasar. One was Karl Barth, the intellectual giant of twentieth-century Protestantism. Barth was nearly twenty years Balthasar's senior, and was already, by the time Balthasar arrived in Basel in 1940, well established as a theological figure, and deeply engaged in the writing of his monumental *Church Dogmatics*. Balthasar had been interested in Barth, and had written about him, before coming to Basel, but the geographical proximity made possible both friendship[14] and a greater intellectual engagement. As well as participating in Barth's seminar on the Council of Trent, Balthasar gave a series of lectures on Barth's theology in 1949-50, lectures which Barth himself sometimes attended.

The engagement with Barth was important on several levels. Out of the lecture series, first of all, came a major book, *The Theology of Karl Barth: Exposition and Interpretation*,[15] in which Balthasar attempted both to set out what was at the heart of Barth's work and to offer a Catholic response to it. From an ecumenical point of view, this book was, for its time, unusual: Balthasar does not wholly endorse Barth's theology, but he writes with a kind of sympathy, admiration, and genuine engagement which was not then characteristic of Catholic/Protestant dialogue.[16] And even if one sets aside the ecumenical dimension, simply as a contribution to the understanding of Karl Barth's thought the book has been very influential. Barth himself seems to have endorsed it, and for a long time Balthasar's diagnosis of the *development* of Barth's thought shaped the way the latter was read.[17]

The engagement with Barth was also important in forming Baltha-

14. Balthasar was a gifted musician, and a shared interest in music — and Mozart in particular — was one of the things that brought them together.

15. San Francisco: Ignatius Press, 1992. It was originally published in 1951.

16. Something which *was* characteristic of Catholic-Protestant encounters of the time was the fact that Balthasar's ultimate goal in engaging with Barth was to see him convert to Roman Catholicism.

17. This is no longer so much the case. Some forty-five years later Bruce McCormack published *Karl Barth's Critically Realistic Dialectical Theology: Its Genesis and Development 1909-1986* (Oxford: Clarendon Press, 1997), in large part to argue for a revision to Balthasar's reading.

sar's own thinking. In a number of ways Balthasar can be seen as a "Barthian" theologian, as echoing Barth's emphases, themes, sensibilities. Like Barth's, Balthasar's theology is marked by Christocentrism, by an emphasis on the distinctiveness, the particularity of revelation, and by a highly critical stance towards modes of thought characteristic of the Enlightenment and modernity. Like Barth, Balthasar lays emphasis on God's prevenience and sovereignty, with a concern to defend this against any possible self-assertion on our part. Like Barth, Balthasar is concerned with the relation between the form and the content of theology, and like Barth he breaks with established patterns in presenting his work.[18] And finally, like Barth, Balthasar is concerned with divine beauty and the beauty of revelation; this is a theme which becomes much more explicitly central in Balthasar, but he himself acknowledges that he is developing something he finds in Barth.

Even where there are divergences, it is possible to see the influence of Barth on Balthasar's thought. One of Balthasar's most famous criticisms of Barth is of Christomonism: Balthasar complains that in Barth's thought all action is so focused on Christ that there seems to be no room left for anyone else, no significance to human response or lack of it, no place for the Church.[19] At the same time, however, Balthasar broadly approves of Barth's Christocentrism, and his emphasis on the priority, prevenience, and sovereignty of God. How then can one maintain these things without falling into Barth's Christological constriction? As we shall see in later chapters, it is possible to understand

18. Thus, for instance, Barth places the doctrine of the Trinity in the prolegomenon to his theology, rather than leaving it to appear at some advanced stage in the presentation of the doctrine of God, or even, as with Schleiermacher, in the appendix; likewise, Balthasar provocatively begins his magnum opus with aesthetics, rather than leaving this, as would be expected, to a final stage of reflection, after what one might call "the solid stuff" had been done.

19. Rodney Howsare's succinct articulation of the issue is admirable here: "If Balthasar appreciated Barth's attempt to think all problems in the light of Christ . . . he worried about Barth's tendency to denigrate the natural in the light of the supernatural. Because in Jesus Christ a full humanity flourishes along with a full divinity — without confusion, without separation — there is no need on the part of the Christian to rob the human (natural) in order to pay the divine (supernatural)." See his *Balthasar: A Guide for the Perplexed* (London and New York: T&T Clark, 2009), p. 25.

some of the distinctive elements of Balthasar's thought precisely as answers to this question.

Adrienne von Speyr

If it was somewhat unusual for a Catholic theologian of Balthasar's generation to be influenced by a Protestant figure like Barth, the second influence that he came under in Basel was still more unusual. This was Adrienne Kaegi von Speyr, a Protestant francophone Swiss doctor. Balthasar met her in 1940, and received her into the Catholic Church in the same year. He acted as her spiritual director, and together with her in 1944 or 1945 founded the *Johannesgemeinschaft*, the Community of St. John. Initially the community was founded for "lay" women,[20] but it was envisaged as including, and did eventually extend to, a branch for "lay" men and one for priests. Those who join these communities take vows of poverty, chastity, and obedience, and undergo a period of formation, but they continue to work in a secular profession, and do not make their membership in the community public.[21] The Community of St. John was eventually to be classed as a "secular institute," a relatively new category in canon law.

Balthasar's commitment to this work with von Speyr, which he understood as a divinely given mission, turned out to be irreconcilable with his continued membership in the Society of Jesus, and in 1950, after four difficult years of discussion and struggle, Balthasar left the Jesuits.

20. Balthasar and others speak of community members as "lay": I use quotation marks here because there is some debate around the question of how helpful it is to apply this term to those who take vows of poverty, chastity, and obedience. Cf. Karl Rahner, "The Layman and the Religious Life: On the Theology of the Secular Institutes," in *Mission and Grace: Essays in Pastoral Theology*, Volume 2 (London and New York: Sheed and Ward, 1964), for a longer discussion of the question.

21. The "hidden" nature of the community's work in the world seems to have been important to the conception of it formed by Balthasar and von Speyr, and so it should perhaps come as no surprise that it is a little difficult to pin down exactly what the purpose of this newly formed community was. Some indications of its general shape are given in Hans Urs von Balthasar, *Our Task: A Report and a Plan*, trans. John Saward (San Francisco: Ignatius, 1994). The original date of publication was 1984.

In the last forty years it has become quite familiar for people to leave religious orders for one reason or another after having taken their vows, but in the middle of the twentieth century this was a more difficult thing to do by far, and carried a heavy stigma. In leaving the Jesuits Balthasar put himself in a position that was, from a social, ecclesiastical, and financial point of view, extremely difficult. He worked as a freelance lecturer to earn his keep, and he felt obliged to leave Basel, whose bishop did not support him. He could not indeed initially find any bishop who would accept him as part of a diocese, and was not formally incardinated into a diocese until 1956. In the 1960s, when the Second Vatican Council was called, Balthasar stood alone among his generation of great theological minds in *not* being invited.

In 1956, at the point when Balthasar was given a degree of ecclesiastical standing by being incardinated into the diocese of Chur, he returned to Basel and took up residence in the home of von Speyr and her second husband, Professor Werner Kaegi, where he lived until von Speyr's death in 1967. Over the years he devoted an enormous level of energy to his work with and for her. This included, as we have seen, the founding of the Community of St. John, for which she acted as the Superior and he as spiritual director. Balthasar also served as a kind of scribe for von Speyr, taking dictation from her, and then editing and publishing her work, which amounted to well over sixty volumes, including those he published posthumously. He in fact founded a publishing house, *Johannes Verlag*, in the first instance precisely in order to be able to publish her works, and he had to subsidize these volumes through earnings from other labors.

In subsequent years Balthasar was very concerned that von Speyr should receive recognition in the Church. Shortly after her death, he produced a small book entitled *A First Glance at Adrienne von Speyr*, which detailed among other things an extraordinary range of visions and experiences. These include, on Balthasar's account, the miraculous cures of some of her patients;[22] the foreknowledge of the death of both her father

---

22. As Balthasar puts it, "sudden, inexplicable cures which were the talk of the town." See *First Glance at Adrienne von Speyr*, trans. Antje Lawry and Sergia Englund, O.C.D. (San Francisco: Ignatius, 1981), p. 34.

and her first husband; a vision of Mary surrounded by angels in her teen years, from which time she always had a small wound under the left breast, over her heart; the ability to bi-locate, so that she would find herself in some place where she was needed, whether a concentration camp, a convent, in the Curia or in a confessional; the reception of the stigmata; a vision of events described in the book of Revelation (11:19-12:3) though she had never read that book. In 1941, after a warning from an angel that "Now it will soon begin," and in each Holy Week subsequently, she had an experience of the Passion, ending on Good Friday at about 3 o'clock in the afternoon "with a death like trance into which flashed the thrust of the lance." During these experiences she shared in new ways each year the suffering of Christ, revealing "a landscape of pain of undreamt-of variety." These sufferings were each year followed by an experience of the "descent into Hell," which would last until early in the morning of Easter Sunday.[23]

One of the more unusual of the things that Balthasar tells us — unusual even within the context of mystics — was von Speyr's capacity to have an experience of the saints. She was able, as he explains it, to share in the experience of the prayer-life of a particular saint, even one of whom she had never heard, and then report to him in some detail what it was like. Altogether she produced approximately 250 brief portraits. For the most part it was Balthasar who directed her towards the investigation of a particular saint: once he had suggested a name, he tells us, "a short prayer would 'transport' Adrienne into the 'ecstasy of obedience'";[24] a short prayer would bring her back to this world. While in this

---

23. Elsewhere, Balthasar tells us that von Speyr had her physical virginity "restored to her by the Lord" (p. 67). He links this in a rather striking way with an area of his own theological interest: "The other theme in this master's [Origen's] work which fascinated me was his repeatedly expressed idea that Christ came upon his Bride, the Church, when she was a prostitute (she had fallen from heaven to earth), and that by his redemptive work he was able to change her back into a virgin. I later pursued the theme through the whole of patristic literature in a larger study and assembled the texts under the title — taken from St. Ambrose — of *Casta Meretrix*. I had no idea, when I was doing this work, that one day what I was describing would be fulfilled in an unfathomable way in the married Adrienne. In this way, she would truly be *personam ecclesiae gerens*, as the Fathers say." *Our Task*, p. 41.

24. *First Glance*, p. 74.

state of ecstasy, she would produce a description of the saint in question, and could, if asked, provide answers to supplementary questions.

With St. Ignatius of Loyola, the sixteenth-century founder of the Jesuits, von Speyr had a particularly close relationship. He first appeared to her, according to Balthasar, when von Speyr was six, and he seemed to be frequently present and instructing her. One illustration of this, which also opens a window onto the complexity of the relationship between Balthasar and von Speyr, has to do with the setting of penance. Von Speyr undertook, Balthasar tells us, a number of severe penances, and she did so apparently at the direction of "heaven," or more specifically of St. Ignatius. Ignatius also seems to have directed, however, that Balthasar himself should be involved in the setting of the penances, so that von Speyr could achieve "absolute ecclesial obedience." Concretely, Adrienne received instructions "from heaven," communicated them to Balthasar, and then "under obedience" could completely forget them.[25] Balthasar in turn would be required to impose these penances "with authority," he writes, sometimes turning himself into "sheer authority" in a way that made it "experientially clear that the obedience of the Church can and at times must have all the reality and the relentlessness of the Cross itself."[26] If he failed to impose the penances exactly as described, he would be required (by St. Ignatius) to start again. On one occasion, near the end of her life, Balthasar was summoned back from a holiday by Adrienne because "some more vigorous practices of penance were required."[27]

I have dwelt a little on what Balthasar reports of the visions and experiences of von Speyr in order to give some sense of the *kind* of influence she might have had on him. On the face of it, one might not expect a person who was almost entirely untrained theologically — who indeed

25. Balthasar does not explain precisely what "under obedience" means, or how this state was achieved. From the way he uses the phrase, however, it is easy to form the impression that it is a kind of sacred analogue to being "under hypnosis": under obedience, memories could be suppressed or restored; von Speyr could return to the state of consciousness she had as a child or teenager; she could be brought into and out of the state by a short prayer.

26. *First Glance*, p. 70.

27. *First Glance*, p. 45. For a critical take on this kind of interaction, cf. Tina Beattie's *New Catholic Feminism: Theology and Theory* (London and New York: Routledge, 2006).

avoided reading too much of the Bible before commenting on any part of it[28] — to be a major influence on Balthasar alongside the likes of de Lubac and Barth. Or again, if one reads that this was someone whom Balthasar received into the Roman Catholic Church, and for whom he acted as spiritual director and confessor, one might suppose that fundamentally the influence would go in the other direction, from him to her. Ultimately, of course, it may not be possible to determine exactly how much influence flowed in each direction. But if one considers Balthasar's description of the range and extraordinary character (even by the standards of previous mystics) of her experiences, as well as the enormous effort he put into taking dictation and publishing her work, and again the way in which he allowed the requirements she made of him, or that God made of him through her, to completely unsettle, indeed to destabilize, the pattern of his life, it is hard to avoid the conclusion that she and her visions and other experiences were of considerable significance in both his life and his thought.

It is not unheard of for theologians in the Catholic tradition to look to the writings of the mystics as a theological source. What the mystics describe is never thought to constitute a new revelation, but it can nevertheless be taken as a source of possible insight, or a locus to which one might turn to confirm a line of thought. Something rather uncommon in Balthasar's case, however, is his *proximity* to his theological source. Balthasar is influenced by, and in some cases makes appeal to the experiences, not of someone whose visions and writings have been sifted and over time received as authentic by the Church, but to someone in whose house he lived and with whom he himself was closely involved — as the one who guided her into the Church, as spiritual director, as scribe, editor, publisher, co-founder of an order, and so on.[29] We will return at the end of this chapter to the question of how this uncommon pattern,

---

28. "And since I started work on the commentaries I have read very little in Scripture. I have to remain open for God. I do not want to be like a bride who reads all kinds of love stories in order to learn how to receive her bridegroom. I do not want to forestall God." *A First Glance*, p. 148. Balthasar presents this as part of a series of statements about herself and her relationship to God that von Speyr made "under obedience."

29. The closeness of their involvement must have been reinforced by the fact that von Speyr could apparently talk of her experiences to no one but Balthasar (*Our Task*, p. 82).

alongside other unusual features of his biography, may have contributed both to the strength of his work and to its weakness.

The period of marginalization resulting from his leaving the Jesuits continued, as we have seen, into the first half of the 1960s. After the Second Vatican Council, however, Balthasar's theological fortunes began to turn. He began to receive various honors — from the University of Edinburgh, for instance, and from the Ecumenical patriarch — and in 1969 he became a member of the Roman Catholic Church's International Theological Commission. In the early 1970s he was involved in founding the international journal *Communio.* By the time he died in 1988 there could be no doubt about the restoration of his status or his influence: he was on the point of being invested as a cardinal, a telegram from Pope John Paul II was read out at his funeral describing him as "a great son of the Church, an outstanding man of theology and of the arts," and his funeral homily was delivered by Cardinal Ratzinger (later, of course, to become Pope Benedict XVI).

Writings

At all stages of his life, whatever his frustrations, whatever his difficulties, and whatever his theological fortunes, Balthasar was a prolific writer. It is important, however, before we turn to a consideration of the range of his writings, to note that Balthasar did not expend what one might call his literary energies only on his own theology; he also was extraordinarily active in translating, anthologizing, editing, and publishing the works of other thinkers. In part this was a matter of making available to the contemporary Church the writings of the Church Fathers. So, for instance, Balthasar produced a substantial anthology of texts translated from Origen, another volume of excerpts from Gregory of Nyssa's *Homilies on the Song of Songs,* a collection of texts from Irenaeus, a selection and translation (but also rearrangement) of Basil of Caesarea's "Rules," a selection of excerpts from the second-century Greek apologists, and a number of translations of excerpts from Augustine. He also translated a number of (entire) works of Maximus the Confessor.[30] But it was not

30. Cf. Brian E. Daley's "Balthasar's Reading of the Church Fathers," in *The Cambridge Companion to Hans Urs von Balthasar,* ed. Edward T. Oakes, S.J., and David Moss (Cam-

only this sort of "ressourcement" — of returning to the "sources" of the theology of the Fathers — that Balthasar involved himself in. He published translations into German of French literature, and a range of more modern anthologies — of the work of Goethe, Novalis, Nietzsche, Brentano, and Borchardt. Additionally, there was the enormous labor of producing the many volumes from Adrienne von Speyr's dictation.

It is perhaps surprising, given all this activity in translating, editing, anthologizing — and even in taking dictation — that Balthasar in fact had any time or strength left for his own writing, but he was also extremely prolific in his own right. From his Ph.D. thesis there eventually emerged a three-volume work, *Apocalypse of the German Soul.* In the 1940s and 50s Balthasar produced a range of monographs on individual figures — Origen, Maximus, Gregory of Nyssa, Thérèse of Lisieux, Elizabeth of Dijon,[31] Reinhold Schneiders,[32] and, as we have already seen, Karl Barth. Also published in this period were a book of aphorisms in 1944 and a freely, almost feverishly written meditation in 1945 entitled *Heart of the World;* a book on the laity in relation to the religious state in 1948; on the theology of history in 1950; on the Church and the need to overcome a fortress mentality in 1952; on prayer in 1955; on "the God question and modern man" in 1956, and so on.[33]

Beginning in 1961, and continuing until 1987, Balthasar produced the trilogy for which he has come to be best known. The first part, *The Glory of the Lord: A Theological Aesthetics,* in seven volumes, emerged between 1961 and 1969. Next came *Theo-Drama: Theological Dramatic Theory,* in five volumes, between 1973 and 1983. The third and final part is the *Theo-Logic,* in three volumes, from 1985 until 1987 (the first of these last three was, however, a reissue of a monograph Balthasar had written nearly

---

bridge: Cambridge University Press, 2004), for a more detailed account of these various translations and anthologies of patristic works.

31. Also known as Elizabeth of the Trinity, she was a Carmelite nun who died young in 1906 and has since been beatified.

32. Reinhard Schneiders (1903-1958) was a friend of Balthasar, a poet, and a Nazi-resister.

33. Peter Henrici suggests that a number of Balthasar's works, including the monographs on Thérèse of Lisieux and Elizabeth of Dijon, on Schneiders and on Bernanos, can be seen as "revolving around Adrienne's mission" ("Sketch of His Life," p. 32).

forty years earlier). These fifteen volumes come to a total of well over 7,000 pages. Once again, it is necessary to observe that this is not all Balthasar was doing during these years. There were also a large number of smaller, occasional, often popular, and sometimes (especially from the middle of the 1960s) quite polemical works. There are five volumes of collected essays under the title *Explorations in Theology* beginning in 1960, more popularly oriented essays in collections such as *Elucidations, New Elucidations,* and *Convergences,* a brief volume entitled *Love Alone: The Way of Revelation,* which forms one of the best entry points into his writing, and a good deal more. Best known among Balthasar's more polemical writings is the volume entitled *Cordula, oder der Ernstfall,* translated into English as *The Moment of Christian Witness,* which contains an attack on Karl Rahner's notion of anonymous Christians. Near the end of his life he entered into controversy on a different front over the question of universal salvation with his *Dare We Hope "That All Men Be Saved"?*

Style

While the sheer quantity of Balthasar's writings makes difficult anything like a general summary of *what* he said, it is more possible to speak in a general way about *how* he said it. We might perhaps distinguish two styles in Balthasar's writings — that of his more popular essays, intended for a broad audience within the Church, and that of his weightier volumes.

When it comes to the popular writings the first thing that must be said is that Balthasar, unlike many other theologians, is adept at writing for a broad audience. His essays are presented in a distinctively non-academic idiom: he assumes, indeed, a kind of intimacy with the reader, rather in the manner of a speaker at a retreat. Even when short, these texts are often directed towards inculcating a global orientation in his readers, a particular posture, a particular ecclesial spirit. Shifting of attitudes or the inculcation of a particular ethos is always more to the fore than, say, unpacking a problem or confronting an intellectual difficulty.

At times this effort is coupled with rather unflattering generalizations about those, especially those theologians, who lack the desired orientation. Balthasar writes, for instance, that Christian people justifiably fear that the "one thing necessary" may be "blocked off and made inaccessible by the 'experts'" or those who pose as experts, those who must often, he writes, "shout so loud in order to justify to themselves their inner predicament of no longer being able to pray."[34] In an essay on lay theologians, he suggests that a considerable portion of these are men "who in reality have a vocation to the priesthood but hold back in fear for a hundred secondary reasons." Such "pseudo-laymen" stifle their vocation by recourse to slogans about "'increasing secularization,' 'urgent need for the lay apostolate,' 'universal priesthood' . . . 'decentralization of the hierarchy,' 'democratization of Church structures.'"[35] One might say that in his popular essays Balthasar is engaged not only in inculcating a global orientation towards faith, Church, and the gospel, but also in inoculating his readers against what he takes to be dangerous trends in the post–Vatican II church.

If directness and a certain intimacy with his readers characterize many of Balthasar's shorter essays, his more substantial works by contrast are often notable for their *indirection*. To read Balthasar in these

34. *Convergences: To the Source of Christian Mystery,* trans. E. A. Nelson (San Francisco: Ignatius, 1983), p. 14. In *A Short Primer for Unsettled Laymen,* trans. Mary Theresilde Skerry (San Francisco: Ignatius, 1985), Balthasar suggests that only a "small number of theologians . . . seek to maintain the true center" (p. 17); he hints that many in the years running up to the Council suffered from something like a loss of faith, so that the reforms suggested at Vatican II "were not seriously considered but immediately overrun and used as a pretext for trampling down what one had long since secretly become weary of" (pp. 16-17); he uses "liberal" in simple contrast with "truly faithful" (p. 41); and he writes of demands for reinterpretation as "a very effective hideout of liberal-rationalist theologizing" (p. 42). Whatever one thinks of the truth of each of these points, the polemical tone is hard to miss.

35. *New Elucidations,* trans. Sister Mary Theresilde Skerry (San Francisco: Ignatius, 1986), p. 199. More generally, Balthasar quite often adopts a rather contemptuous tone towards those with whom he is in theological disagreement. In the *Epilogue* to his trilogy, for instance, after an evocation of the state of American and European youth, he asks "where is the famous 'point of contact' with the *anima technica vacua?*" How, he is asking, can one do theology for people who are formed by constant television watching? Balthasar's answer is despairing, but what is most striking about it is the way he treats one of the most significant theological movements of the second half of the twentieth century: "I for one certainly do not know. Some table-rapping, a séance or two, some dabbling in Zen meditation, a smattering of *liberation theology:* enough." *Epilogue,* trans. Edward T. Oakes, S.J. (San Francisco: Ignatius, 2004), p. 11, emphasis added.

works is very often to embark on a tour of a vast theological, philosophical, and literary landscape, not always sure what the point of the tour is or where it is taking one. In some cases, of course, it is clear from the outset that the focus will be on exposition and exploration of the thought of another. Balthasar produced, as we have seen, numerous monographs focused on individual thinkers; two out of the seven volumes of *The Glory of the Lord* are devoted to studies of a dozen figures from the Christian tradition — specifically the "theological styles" of figures ranging from Irenaeus and Augustine to Soloviev, Hopkins, and Péguy. But very often in Balthasar's works even when the overall focus is thematic, one finds oneself whisked from thinker to thinker and century to century. One might take as typical a thirty-five-page passage of *The Truth of God* (*Theo-Logic* 2), for instance, in which one finds discussed Maurice Blondel, G. W. F. Hegel, Paul Claudel, St. Augustine of Hippo, Richard of St. Victor, Martin Buber, Franz Rosenzweig, Ferdinand Ebner, and Matthias Scheeben. Nor is Balthasar simply *referring* to these figures in the course of setting out a position; rather, he sets out, or arrives at, the position precisely *through* the (rather breathless) series of discussions.

The expository dimension of Balthasar's writing can be seen partly in the context of the *ressourcement* that de Lubac and others were engaged in. Partly, that is to say, Balthasar engaged in extended expository projects in order to make available, and give renewed prominence to, certain figures and patterns of thought from the tradition, and thus to reshape the contemporary Church. In this respect his expository works stand in continuity with the extensive editing, translating, and publishing labors he undertook — and even in continuity with his immense efforts to make public the work of Adrienne von Speyr. De Lubac influenced Balthasar's cohort of students at Fourvières by giving them access to the notes and extracts from the Fathers he had made; Balthasar, one could say, is trying to do something similar with the Church more broadly — to give his contemporaries access to his notes and extracts from the tradition, literary and philosophical as well as theological, and thus in some way to bring about a shift in the contemporary theological horizon.

One cannot account for the characteristic indirection of Balthasar's writing entirely with reference to the project of *ressourcement,* however.

At times, especially when the pace at which he moves from one figure to the next is particularly dizzying, it seems more appropriate to attribute this simply to the cast of his own mind. Balthasar was immensely learned, and was inclined to work out his thought in relation to broad-ranging surveys of thinkers. He had an impulse toward comprehensive-ness, we might say — the significance of which we will return to in later chapters.

Reception

We have already seen that Balthasar was in a profoundly difficult posi-tion following his departure from the Jesuits in 1950, and that while de Lubac, Rahner, Schillebeeckx, Ratzinger, Congar, Lonergan, Küng, and hundreds of other theologians were invited to the Second Vatican Council (1962-5), Balthasar stayed at home. In the 1950s and early 60s he was decidedly outside the theological mainstream, a marginalized voice.

The change in Balthasar's theological fortunes has been profound. At his death, Balthasar was on the point of being made a cardinal. The Pope at the time, John Paul II, wrote in a funeral telegram of the "high es-teem" in which the Holy See held both Balthasar and his life's work, and described him as "a great son of the Church, an outstanding man of the-ology and of the arts." The future Pope, Joseph Cardinal Ratzinger, deliv-ering the homily at his funeral, heaped praise on the spirit animating his work, and explained his being named to the cardinalate as a kind of for-mal stamp of approval on his theology: "the Church itself, in its official responsibility, tells us that he is right in what he teaches of the Faith, that he points the way to the sources of living water."[36]

Since his death, Balthasar's standing has continued to grow, perhaps especially in the English-speaking world. An extensive, and mostly adulatory, secondary literature has grown up around him, and continues to expand rapidly. Many of his writings have been translated into English and are currently in print — something which could not be said for some

---

36. Joseph Cardinal Ratzinger, "Homily at the Funeral Liturgy of Hans Urs von Balthasar," in Schindler, ed., *Life and Work*, p. 295.

of the other major Catholic theologians of the twentieth century. One can read on the back of some recently printed editions Pope Benedict describing Balthasar as an "authoritative guide" and the publisher affirming that he was "one of the greatest theologians of the twentieth century, perhaps of all time."

Balthasar's influence and standing is not only an inner-Catholic affair. One can find strong interest in him in a post-liberal thinker like George Lindbeck, in the early stages at least of the Radical Orthodoxy movement, in Donald MacKinnon, an enormously influential Anglican theologian of the previous generation, and in Rowan Williams, an enormously influential Anglican theologian of our own generation. At the moment, if a Protestant or Anglican wishes, in an ecumenical spirit, to engage with one Roman Catholic thinker, it is almost certainly Balthasar who will be chosen.

Why such a reversal of fortunes? There are a number of things to consider. First, against the backdrop of the turmoil the Roman Catholic Church underwent in the 1960s, Balthasar's leaving the Jesuits began to seem of less consequence than once it had. Second, Balthasar's magnum opus began to appear: the initial volume of *The Glory of the Lord* was published in 1961, and by the end of the decade the whole of this first part of the trilogy was complete. Then, too, the significance of his more polemical work should perhaps not be underestimated. *The Moment of Christian Witness,* an attack on the direction theology and church were moving in the aftermath of the Council, and particularly on Rahner's notion of anonymous Christians, appeared in 1966. Balthasar emerged, then, both as a heavyweight theologian with a major creative project, and as a writer who could forcefully articulate concerns about the direction in which the contemporary Church was moving. For those within Roman Catholicism who worried that the Church was conceding too much to the world, to the secular, to "the times," and that it was in danger of losing its identity, Balthasar became a very important figure. At his funeral Cardinal Ratzinger described the journal *Communio* as "a powerful source for correct renewal as opposed to its counterfeit forms":[37] Balthasar was a leading figure in founding *Communio,* but the phrase

37. Ibid., p. 294.

might also be taken as a description of what Balthasar's work as a whole represented for some parts of the Catholic world.

The attractiveness of Balthasar to *non*-Catholic readers is of a slightly different nature. There is, first of all, the fact that Balthasar was influenced by, and already in dialogue with, Karl Barth, while remaining distinctively Roman Catholic. So in his work the ecumenical encounter is already begun. And while Protestant readers may not be so interested in his critique of trends in post–Vatican II Roman Catholicism, they are very interested in the much broader criticism of modernity that weaves its way through his writings. Balthasar can be read, that is to say, as a postmodern theologian, as a resource in escaping from the shackles of the Enlightenment. And in particular, Balthasar's turn to poetry and drama — to literature as a theological source — has had enormous appeal.

Unfettered

If Hans Urs von Balthasar is now received with great respect, at times even with reverence, it is still important to remember that this has not always been the case, and in particular that this was not the case during the major portion of his writing career. And it is perhaps worth asking, how does a theologian's position, whether at the center or at the margins of Church and academia, shape, or at least inflect, the way he does theology? If one finds oneself, in spite of education, ability, and prior background, very much on the margins of the Church, an outsider with respect to power, influence, and respectability, could it be that one's writing is shaped less by a sense of decorum and caution, of the need for judicious balance, and more by insistence, forcefulness, daring, the need to be heard? Could it be, that is to say, that one might react to the lack of power and authority in one's circumstances by developing a literary and theological voice which assumes a great deal of authority?

If this is the case, then it is, I would suggest, one of a number of factors in Balthasar's biography that contribute towards making him something of an *unfettered* theologian. Another such factor is his education. Mark Twain is supposed to have advised never to let one's schooling get in the way of one's education, and, as we have seen, there seem to have been echoes of such a philosophy in the approach Balthasar took towards his formal philosophical and theological studies. If one considers his utter disdain for neo-scholasticism, the wax in the ears, and the many other intellectual paths he followed during his years of formal intellectual formation, one might regard him, on a theological and philosophical level, as something of an autodidact.[38]

The fact that Balthasar never held an academic post is also worth considering in this connection. Someone who teaches in a university or a seminary typically works in relatively close proximity with colleagues who know more about a whole variety of things than he or she does — so that I, for instance, as a systematic theologian, am aware of those alongside whom I work who know more about the Bible and the state of biblical scholarship than I, colleagues who know far more Church history than I, colleagues who know far more about Judaism and Islam than I, colleagues in departments next door who know more about the state of philosophy, or literature, or classics, than I, and so on. Balthasar, throughout his writing career, had no such colleagues. He worked out of the house of Adrienne von Speyr and her husband, founding a new community, founding indeed his own publishing house. Such a context must undoubtedly have been very challenging, and must have required heroic levels of work and energy, but it was also a context in which there were no intellectual restraints from any side to affect what he wrote — no colleagues or students to hold him intellectually accountable, no religious order to which he must answer, no publisher to raise a query.

The unfettered quality of Balthasar's work, to which so many factors in his biography seem to have contributed, is on the one hand one of its great strengths. There is a freshness of approach, to give one example, in the way he organizes his vast trilogy into aesthetics, dramatics, and logic, which could perhaps never have been achieved had he been a diligent student of neo-scholasticism, or had his thought been shaped by the necessities of delivering fixed cycles of lectures to students. Or again, his theology of Holy Saturday, influenced as it clearly was by von Speyr's experiences, would surely never have been written had his life followed a

---

38. In this context it is worth remembering that his biggest influence during these years was Henri de Lubac, himself a theological autodidact.

more predictable pattern. Contemporary theology has been in various ways enriched precisely *because* Balthasar was such an unfettered theologian, able to open up genuinely fresh possibilities for theological reflection.

At the same time, however, this unfettered quality is, I think, the greatest danger in Balthasar's thought. It can give rise to a theology which often goes too far, which knows and asserts too much, which argues too little, which has a persistent tendency to exceed all bounds — a theology, indeed, that does not seem to hold itself accountable to Scripture, tradition, or its readers, but somehow soars above them all.

CHAPTER 3

Central Images 1: The Picture and the Play

Balthasar's work is so broad-ranging, as I have already suggested, as to defy summary; in any case it certainly defies summary in a single volume.[1] One strategy in the face of this difficulty is to focus on a certain number of select themes that one might present as the core of his thought, or at least themes with which a reader wanting to grapple with him ought to begin. A number of very helpful and interesting introductions to Balthasar have indeed followed this strategy.[2] The approach here will be slightly different. I will begin by looking, not at key themes, but at central images and patterns of thought. The goal of this volume is

1. For an attempt at something like a comprehensive *multi*-volume summary, or at least guide, see the books of Aidan Nichols: *Scattering the Seed: A Guide through Balthasar's Early Writings on Philosophy and the Arts* (New York and London: T&T Clark, 2006); *The Word Has Been Abroad: A Guide Through Balthasar's Aesthetics* (Edinburgh: T&T Clark, 1998); *No Bloodless Myth: A Guide Through Balthasar's Dramatics* (Edinburgh: T&T Clark, 1999); *Say It Is Pentecost: A Guide Through Balthasar's Logic* (Edinburgh: T&T Clark, 2001); *Divine Fruitfulness: A Guide Through Balthasar's Theology Beyond the Trilogy* (Edinburgh: T&T Clark, 2007).

2. Most recently, a very impressive job has been done by Rodney A. Howsare in his *Balthasar: A Guide for the Perplexed* (London and New York: T&T Clark, 2009). Cf. also the helpful introductions by O'Donnell and Oakes: John O'Donnell, S.J., *Hans Urs von Balthasar,* Outstanding Christian Thinkers Series (London and New York: Continuum, 1991); Edward T. Oakes, S.J., *Pattern of Redemption: The Theology of Hans Urs von Balthasar* (New York: Continuum, 2002). Kevin Mongrain's *The Systematic Thought of Hans Urs von Balthasar: An Irenaean Retrieval* (New York: Crossroad, 2002) makes an interesting argument for interpreting Balthasar through the lens of (Balthasar's reading of) Irenaeus, but also provides a helpful introduction to Balthasar's thought.

not just to lay out for the reader some of the things that Balthasar said, some of the content of his theology, but to get a certain purchase on his thought as a whole, on its shape and style, its proclivities and dangers. For this purpose, approaching it from a rather unusual angle — from a consideration of central images and recurring patterns of thought — will prove helpful.

In this chapter, in particular, I will consider two images that Balthasar very deliberately chooses to make pivotal. Each of these sits at the center of, and becomes a kind of focus of, its own massive, multi-volume project (the first and second parts of Balthasar's trilogy, respectively). While I shall not attempt to summarize the content of these two sprawling works,[3] consideration of these images and the way they function will allow us to make a certain foray into the projects in which they are embedded.

Transfixed: Seeing the Form

First, then, we must imagine a spectator standing transfixed before a great work of art — a painting, perhaps, or a statue — who is caught up, taken out of himself or herself, by its beauty. This is the image at the heart of the first part of Balthasar's trilogy, the seven-volume *Glory of the Lord: A Theological Aesthetics*.

In principle, it should be said, Balthasar is interested, in *The Glory of the Lord*, with beauty and the perception of it *in general*, and not just with the phenomenon of seeing a beautiful piece of art. Things other than

---

3. They do not in fact, in my judgment, particularly lend themselves to summary. This is in part because Balthasar himself works so much through commentary upon and selective summaries of vast numbers of other authors. The would-be summarizer needs either to give still more condensed summaries of those whom Balthasar treats, or else to attempt to make Balthasar's points much more directly than he himself was willing to do. The latter approach, though it can be helpful to readers, inevitably moves summary in the direction of a quite selective interpretation. Whether a summary of the first kind can in fact have any hope of giving the reader a grasp of what is going on in Balthasar is very much an open question. For an attempt, see two of the volumes by Aidan Nichols mentioned in note 1 above, *The Word Has Been Abroad* and *No Bloodless Myth*. A relatively brief guide to the trilogy as a whole is offered by Stephen Wigley in his recent *Balthasar's Trilogy* (New York and London: T&T Clark, 2010).

works of art can be beautiful, and beauty can be perceived in other ways than through seeing. There is the beauty of the flower, or the beauty in a pattern of life — neither of which are works of art, and both of which can be found as examples in Balthasar's writing. Or again, there is the beauty of music — an art form, but one that is heard rather than seen — and in personal terms music seems to have been considerably more important to Balthasar than visual art forms. Nevertheless, the image which principally guides his reflection is in fact that of *seeing* a beautiful object, and in particular seeing a beautiful work of art.[4]

Balthasar does not attempt to define beauty, nor does he offer any kind of methodical analysis of what is involved in perceiving it, nor again any careful tracing of the history of ideas such as those of beauty or art. The first volume of *The Glory of the Lord,* subtitled "Seeing the Form," begins, not with any attempt at careful or systematic examination of ideas in aesthetics, but with a variety of ruminations on beauty, the perception of it, and the importance of both. The experience of beauty is for the most part evoked and alluded to rather than described, analyzed, or argued over.

Insofar as Balthasar does nevertheless suggest at times a kind of analysis of the phenomenon of beauty, it is in terms, on the one hand, of form or figure *(Gestalt* or *Gebilde),* and on the other, of splendor, or radiance, or luminosity, or some other term suggestive of light. Thus, for instance, we read:

> Those words which attempt to convey the beautiful gravitate, first of all, toward the mystery of form *(Gestalt)* or of figure *(Gebilde).* *Formosus* ("beautiful") comes from *forma* ("shape") and *speciosus*

4. Edward Oakes, in his *Pattern of Redemption,* emphasizes the importance of music for Balthasar, and the importance of hearing more generally. He argues, drawing primarily on an essay from the second volume of Balthasar's *Explorations in Theology,* that "Hearing is the central theological act of perception" (*Pattern of Redemption,* p. 137). But Oakes then has to grapple with the fact that the first volume of Balthasar's aesthetics is not entitled "*Hearing* the Form" but "*Schau der Gestalt,*" "Seeing the Form." Oakes resolves the difficulty by suggesting that when what is seen is in fact the beautiful, seeing becomes much more like hearing, particularly in that it is no longer in control. We are still, however, left with the fact that, in Balthasar's *Theological Aesthetics,* the fundamental guiding image is that of seeing a work of art.

("comely") from *species* ("likeness"). But this is to raise the question of the "great radiance from within" which transforms *species* into *speciosa:* the question of *splendour.* We are confronted simultaneously with both the figure and that which shines forth from the figure.[5]

To experience beauty, as Balthasar presents it to us, is to be able to see the form, the *Gestalt,* of that which is beautiful, and to see it *as* radiant, as lit up. Of particular importance to Balthasar's thinking, furthermore, is an insistence on where the light in question comes from:

> the light does not fall on this form [which the beautiful is] from above and from outside, rather it breaks forth from the form's interior.[6]

The beautiful does not owe its beauty to something external to itself, and certainly not to the "eye of the beholder." Or to put it another way, form and splendor are not two separate elements which, when they happen to coincide, produce beauty: instead, on Balthasar's account, the one emanates, radiates, from the other.

To speak of beauty in terms of form, *Gestalt,* carries with it at least two significant implications. First there is the fact that the beautiful, as Balthasar presents it, is always determinate: when we perceive the beautiful we are not just overwhelmed by something chaotic, shapeless, amorphous, but we encounter a distinct *form.* We do not meet beauty in general, beauty as an abstraction, but always a particular beautiful thing. The spectator, to go back to our central image, stands in front of some individual piece of art, with its very particular shape and structure, its very particular contours, and finds him or herself caught up in the beauty of that particular work; the experience of beauty is not, that is to say, to be had in any kind of unspecified or indeterminate way. Secondly, the word *Gestalt* brings with it an emphasis (not automatically present in the English term "form") on the *wholeness* of that which is perceived, or on the way its parts or components are brought together into a totality:

---

5. *Glory of the Lord,* Volume 1: *Seeing the Form,* trans. Erasmo Leiva-Merikakis (Edinburgh: T&T Clark, 1982), pp. 19-20.

6. *Seeing the Form,* p. 151.

> Our first principle must always be the indissolubility of form. . . . If
> form is broken down into subdivisions and auxiliary parts for the sake
> of explanation, this is unfortunately a sign that the true form has not
> been perceived as such at all.[7]

To perceive the *Gestalt* of something one has to grasp it, to see it, not
piece by piece, but all at once, as a totality.

The significance of speaking in terms of the splendor, the radiance,
of beauty, is slightly more elusive. Balthasar denies, as we have seen, that
radiance comes from somewhere other than the form, from outside the
form, as it were. But this is not to say that it is then simply and completely identified *with* the form. Balthasar sometimes uses the language
of depth, of something beyond — or beneath — the form, which somehow shines in and through the form.

> The form as it appears to us is beautiful only because the delight that
> it arouses in us is founded upon the fact that, in it, the truth and good-
> ness of the depths of reality itself are manifested and bestowed. . . . We
> "behold" the form; but, if we really behold it, it is not as a detached
> form, rather in its unity with the depths that make their appearance in
> it. We see form as the splendour, as the glory of Being.[8]

What seems to be suggested is that while form is determinate and particular, its splendor arises from the fact that something more — something from the "depths," the "depths of being," the "depths of reality" —
shines through it, and is perceived in it.

Before we turn to the question of what significance all this has for theology, we might pause to ask: is this in fact the way beauty is? This is a kind
of question that Balthasar's writing does not particularly encourage. As we
have seen, Balthasar does not so much analyze or develop arguments
about the nature of beauty as offer wide-ranging ruminations; in the
course of these ruminations, the concept of beauty that emerges is presented not as *one* conception of beauty which might perhaps be argued to

7. Ibid., p. 26.
8. Ibid., pp. 118-19.

be superior to *other* possible conceptions, but rather as an unavoidable account of the way things are. Thus, if one hunts in Balthasar's texts for *reasons* to take form and splendor as the basic coordinates for beauty, the closest one can get to a justification are certain breathtakingly broad generalizations. We have seen that Balthasar makes a claim that "Those words which attempt to convey the beautiful gravitate" to form and splendor, and that, elsewhere, he introduces form and splendor as one way of naming the "two elements in the beautiful which have traditionally controlled *every* aesthetic."[9] Not only does Balthasar introduce his position (even to call it "*his* position" is in a sense to resist the logic of his presentation) with a certain aura of self-evidence and inevitability; he also insists that beauty is the first thing, the "primal phenomenon"[10] — thus fundamentally prior to analysis and argument — and yet generally inadequately *perceived* in the modern world. The would-be questioner, then, very easily finds himself wrong-footed: perhaps if one is not able to acknowledge in all simplicity that beauty is a matter of form and splendor, it is because one has lost the feeling for it, the ability to perceive it, and so has become too concerned to submit to analysis that which one cannot simply *recognize*. It is necessary in some sense to resist the drift of Balthasar's writing, in short, even to pose the question "is this in fact a persuasive way of characterizing beauty?"

One might seek to address the question in a straightforward, naïve way, by simply asking, does this description of beauty in fact fit examples of beauty of which one is aware? Certainly the beauty of some paintings would seem to be well-described in terms of a sense of splendor, a radiance from within; one might think of the luminosity of the domestic scenes of Vermeer, for instance, or a different kind of radiance in a Van Gogh. But would the notion apply to *all* beautiful paintings (and all else that is beautiful)? Or again, can we be sure even that form is always central to beauty? Is it possible to imagine something chaotic and random that is yet beautiful?[11]

9. Ibid., p. 118 (emphasis added).

10. Ibid., p. 20.

11. Might randomly swirling colors, for instance, not sometimes be beautiful? What about the aurora borealis? The defender of Balthasar might reply, of course, that there is still form here, in that the colors are distinct, each themselves, and not all so mingled as to lose their distinctiveness.

One might alternatively approach the question historically, asking whether Balthasar is giving a fair characterization of the history of aesthetics when he presents it as always revolving around the elements of form and splendor. Has it really always been as he says it has always been? A brief glance at more detailed historical treatments of the concept of beauty would seem to suggest that, *if* one restricts oneself to a pre-modern, certainly pre-Kantian, history, one can indeed talk about a long continuity in a theory of beauty. But this is the continuity of a particular dominant theory of beauty which is rather more specific than what Balthasar describes. It is a theory of beauty with a quite specific origin (in Pythagoras) and lineage, which holds not just to a broad concept of beauty as form, but to beauty as something which is apprehended through the mind rather than the senses, which has to do quite specifically with proportion, and which is usually conceived as essentially numerical in character.

To press the question further: might Balthasar in fact be drawing on, and shaped by, not what is common in all experience of beauty and to all ages' understanding of it (or even to all pre-modern ages' understanding of it), but the quite particular sensibility and outlook of a period in the relatively recent past? This would seem a distinct possibility. Nicholas Boyle, for instance, after offering an interesting account of the development of "Art" as a new idea and of an autonomous discipline of aesthetics in eighteenth-century Germany — both as in some way the product of the "secularization of a clerical class" — suggests that the central concepts of Balthasar's *Glory of the Lord,* including his concept of beauty, "derive from, or are profoundly influenced by, the usage of the German classical and romantic, or idealist, generations."[12] If Boyle is right, then we should not necessarily adopt Balthasar's conception of beauty unless

12. Nicholas Boyle, "'Art,' Literature, and Theology: Learning from Germany," in *Higher Learning and Catholic Traditions,* ed. Robert E. Sullivan (Notre Dame: University of Notre Dame Press, 2001), p. 105. "In his understanding of 'aesthetics,' 'Art,' and 'beauty,'" writes Boyle, "Balthasar is, as much as the nineteenth-century sages, the inheritor of the secular gospels of ex-clergymen" (p. 106). His argument as a whole is fascinating, and includes the suggestion that Balthasar's reading of the full historical sweep of western thought is largely shaped by "the internal tensions in the intellectual life of late-eighteenth-century Germany."

we are persuaded that this particular moment in modern German intellectual history really ought to be privileged.

In any case, our main concern here is not ultimately to render a judgment on the adequacy or otherwise of Balthasar's conception of beauty, but to come to grips with the way in which this concept of beauty, and the central image of "seeing the form," give a distinctive style and shape to his theology. We have glanced briefly at the question of whether Balthasar is right about beauty only because some of the issues it raises (the difficulty in putting questions to Balthasar, the way in which he makes, or fails to make, arguments, a certain tendency to present positions as though they have a more obvious universality or a greater self-evidence than may in fact be justified) will recur in later contexts.

How then does this business of the perception of beauty, this image of "seeing the form," standing transfixed before the beauty of a work of art, come to play a central role in Balthasar's theology? The answer, in its simplest form, is that we are to think of God's revelation on the analogy with a work of art, and the act of faith on the analogy of the person who stands before a work of art, gazing upon it and being transported by it. Theology then becomes focused, not on examining or expressing the *truths* of revelation, or on bringing out its coherence, or illuminating its meaningfulness, but instead on expressing and examining the *beauty* of revelation. And so the seven substantial volumes of *The Glory of the Lord* are devoted (in principle at least)[13] to an exploration of the beauty of revelation, a study of revelation from the perspective of its beauty.

This does not mean, it is important to be clear, that Balthasar devotes seven volumes to a discussion of the literary merits of the canonical writings. It is *Christ* who is at the heart of God's revelation, and it is the beauty of the form of Christ — a beauty to which Scripture points, but with which it is not identical — which is, ultimately, the object of all of his theological aesthetics. If Christ is the revelation of God, however, Christ cannot be understood — the "form" of Christ cannot be grasped

---

13. I add "in principle" because it is always dangerous to approach Balthasar expecting him to hold tightly to a single theme, even one so broad as "the confrontation of beauty and revelation" (*Seeing the Form*, p. 9). So much comes into view in Balthasar's larger efforts that it is often better to conceive of them as wide-ranging theological explorations which periodically return to a given theme, rather than as tightly focused studies.

— outside of or apart from all that the revelation of Christ presupposes, outside or apart from his proper context. And this context is very broad: it would include the whole of what is sometimes called "salvation history," the history before Christ traced in the Bible, and even more generally the whole of history as such, the whole of creation. Christ also cannot be grasped, on Balthasar's account, apart from the Church to which he gives rise.

In taking the beauty of revelation as the central focus of the first part of his major trilogy Balthasar is quite self-consciously going against the grain of the times. The modern world, he thinks, has lost touch with beauty, has lost its ability to see and appreciate it, and has lost a sense of its importance:

> Beauty is the disinterested one, without which the ancient world refused to understand itself, a word which both imperceptibly and yet unmistakably has bid farewell to our new world, a world of interests, leaving it to its own avarice and sadness.[14]

In fact, however, to appreciate the force of his theological aesthetics, one needs to notice that Balthasar is not just resisting tendencies of the modern world in some general sense, but that he is rather more concretely going against the grain of neo-scholastic patterns of thought. As we saw in the previous chapter, neo-scholasticism largely controlled the Roman Catholic philosophical and theological world in which Balthasar was educated. Fergus Kerr points out very effectively just how shocking in various ways the first volume of *Herrlichkeit* would have been when first published in 1961, with the Second Vatican Council still unknown and unanticipated, and neo-scholastic dominance still firm.[15] One of the things that would surely have been shocking is the proposal to *start* theology with something as apparently frivolous as aesthetics, with questions of beauty and the issue of perceiving the beauty of the whole of revelation, rather than, in the mode of the rationalist neo-scholastics, with

14. *Seeing the Form,* p. 18.

15. Fergus Kerr, "Foreword: Assessing 'This Giddy Synthesis,'" *Balthasar at the End of Modernity,* by Lucy Gardner, David Moss, Ben Quash, and Graham Ward (Edinburgh: T&T Clark, 1999), pp. 1-13.

carefully developed arguments to demonstrate truths about God that can be known through reason alone, and a further set of arguments to demonstrate the credibility of revelation, i.e., the reasonableness of accepting a second set of truths that cannot be rationally demonstrated.

"Fundamental theology," in Roman Catholic contexts, is a theological subdiscipline which in some sense prepares the way for the rest of theology (i.e., for "dogmatic theology"): it was traditionally understood as establishing the credibility of faith before the actual content of the faith was examined. Balthasar is essentially placing his theological aesthetics in the role of a fundamental theology, of an enquiry into the credibility, the believability, of the faith, but insisting at the same time that this question of credibility cannot be considered apart from the actual content of faith — fundamental theology cannot be done apart from dogmatic theology. And the *route* to credibility, as Balthasar presents it, is not by way of any kind of orderly establishing of truths — that some can be known from first principles and that others can be accepted on appropriate authority — but by drawing attention to the *beauty* of the whole of what is revealed.[16]

Balthasar takes beauty to be one of the "transcendentals," one of the traditional "notes" of being.[17] The implication is that beauty is not something merely frivolous and ornamental, a kind of afterthought, but just as central and fundamental as truth and goodness. If one takes this seriously, then to ask about the beauty of revelation ought to be no less serious than to ask about its truth or its consequences for the way we live our lives. Fur-

---

16. The insistence that fundamental theology cannot be separated from dogmatic theology (which is something like a Roman Catholic version of a rejection of foundationalism) Balthasar shares with Rahner, but in the case of the latter, the credibility of faith is brought about not by an examination of its beauty, but by showing that it can be linked with experience.

17. "Transcendentals" are distinguished by being attributes not just of some beings, but of all. The term goes back to Aristotle (the "transcendentals" transcended his division of beings into ten categories), and took on importance in medieval thought. "Beauty" is in fact a relative late-comer to traditional lists of transcendentals; unity, truth, and goodness are the most consistently named. Transcendentals are spoken of by medieval thinkers as "convertible" with each other and with being — you cannot have any one without the others. Balthasar's trilogy as a whole is focused around the three transcendentals of beauty *(Theological Aesthetics)*, goodness *(Theo-Drama)*, and truth *(Theo-Logic)*.

thermore, suggests Balthasar quite compellingly, without beauty, truth and goodness lose their force: who could in fact ever be brought to give their life to something because of arguments for its truth, if they did not see it as attractive? And if morality, if goodness, lacks beauty, what is to stop us from simply turning away from it in indifference?

To talk of these transcendentals — of truth, beauty, and goodness — is to talk in a general, universal mode. Balthasar is concerned, as one might expect from a theologian who has been influenced by Barth, that with the notion of beauty he not be taken to be imposing any kind of prior system or theoretical program upon revelation. He therefore makes a distinction (in *Seeing the Form,* p. 38) between a "theological aesthetics" and an "aesthetic theology." An aesthetic theology, in contrast to his own project, is what happens when one applies some already-given notion to revelation, thus "betraying and selling out theological substance to the current viewpoints of an inner-worldly theory of beauty." Of course just articulating such a distinction — just contrasting "theological aesthetics" to "aesthetic theology" — does not settle the matter. There is a real intellectual knot here, for Balthasar is committed on the one hand to a "sharp contrast" between worldly and revealed beauty,[18] and on the other hand to an important *analogy* between them:[19] his capacity to coherently negotiate the tension between these two commitments is in fact a key issue running through the whole of the *Theological Aesthetics.*[20]

I will suggest below some possible reservations about Balthasar's programmatic use of the image of seeing and being transfixed by a work of art, but it is important to try to set out somewhat more fully what can

18. "The divine principle of form must in many ways stand in sharp contrast to the beauty of this world" (*Seeing the Form,* p. 38).

19. "It appears impossible to deny that there exists an analogy between God's work of formation and the shaping forces of nature and of man as they generate and give birth" (ibid.).

20. As Noel O'Donaghue puts it, in a review of the first volume of the *Theological Aesthetics,* "a lot of the excitement of the book comes from the tension between the Barthian theology of discontinuity (and the total Otherness of God in Christ) and that Platonic and Aristotelian strand in Catholic theology which sees nature and grace as somehow continuous, and so defends the basic goodness and beauty of human life." See his "A Theology of Beauty," in *The Analogy of Beauty: The Theology of Hans Urs von Balthasar,* ed. John Riches (Edinburgh: T&T Clark, 1986).

make this approach attractive. It allows Balthasar, first of all, to escape a purely propositionalist conception of faith and revelation — whereby faith is simply the believing of a series of truths on God's authority — without thereby losing the sense of the specificity of Christianity, and of its concrete contours. It allows him, indeed, to offer a conception of revelation as containing the genuinely new, the other, even the strange — something that a thinker like Karl Barth is very concerned with — without having to buy this at the price (as Karl Barth can sometimes seem to) of insisting on a deep negation of our nature, or presenting revelation in terms of a fundamental alienation. A work of art can be genuinely new and surprising, can present us with a kind of beauty never previously imagined, and yet still hold us transfixed rather than alienated. Or to put it a different way, Balthasar's image of "seeing the form" allows him to envisage revelation as something that really touches us, that makes a real connection to us, that has a genuine relevance to us (something a thinker like Karl Rahner is very concerned about) without thereby running the risk (as Rahner can sometimes seem to do) of reducing revelation to an expression of our experience, of that which is already within us. A work of art can be genuinely other to us, and yet genuinely make a connection with us.

The emphasis on form and what is involved in perceiving it also allows Balthasar to articulate a fundamental critique of modern biblical criticism, in many of its guises at least. To appreciate a work of art, one needs to perceive its *Gestalt,* to see it as a *whole:* one does not come to understand a painting, for instance, by dividing it into pieces, doing a definitive analysis of each of these pieces, and then amalgamating the individual analyses. Similarly, to appreciate a work of art, one needs to see what is *actually there,* what is given; one does not arrive at an appreciation by going behind the final work to reconstruct the reasons for its creation, the original ingredients out of which the paint was ground, and so on. Such questions may sometimes be relevant to ask, but they cannot be a substitute for the actual contemplation of the finished totality of the work. And so, where Scripture is concerned, Balthasar can insist:

> Only the final result of the historical developments which lie behind a
> text — a history never to be adequately reconstructed — may be said

to be inspired, not the bits and scraps which philological analysis thinks it can tear loose from the finished totality in order, as it were, to steal up to the form from behind in the hope of enticing it to betray its mystery by exposing its development.

Or, in a still stronger vein:

> For we can be sure of one thing: we can never again recapture the living totality of form once it has been dissected and sawed into pieces, no matter how informative the conclusions which this anatomy may bring to light. Anatomy can be practiced only on a dead body, since it is opposed to the movement of life and seeks to pass from the whole to its parts and elements.[21]

If perceiving beauty requires the perception of form, and form essentially has to do with the totality of a work, then an approach to Scripture which systematically pulls the totality apart in order, as it imagines, really to get to the bottom of things, is doomed from the start to miss all that is of most value.[22]

---

21. *Seeing the Form*, p. 31.

22. For some questions about the fairness of Balthasar's treatment of historical criticism, in the context of what is overall a sympathetic reading of his approach to biblical interpretation, see W. T. Dickens, *Hans Urs von Balthasar's* Theological Aesthetics: *A Model for Post-Critical Biblical Interpretation* (Notre Dame: University of Notre Dame Press, 2003). There have been developments in the nature of historical criticism, already underway when Balthasar was writing, which mean that some of his criticism misses the mark: "In light of these changes within the discipline, it is no longer credible, if it ever was, to attack historical criticism on the grounds that it fails to appreciate the complex ways in which the Bible's parts interact with one another" (p. 78). Dickens also raises interesting questions about Balthasar's insistence that a historical criticism which does not work from the perspective of faith cannot perceive "the internal harmony of the form of revelation in its biblical mediation": "it does not seem unreasonable to contend that a nonbeliever can recognize the harmony of relations seen by a Christian without believing that Jesus is the Son of God. Just as a Christian can come to see the beauty of the *Bhagavad-Gita's* theological synthesis of the ways of knowledge, action, and devotion without believing Krishna to be Lord of the cosmos, a Hindu can learn to appreciate the internal harmony of relations among the forms of salvation history as they coalesce around Jesus without accepting him as the Christ" (p. 75).

Balthasar's approach makes possible an emphasis on the specificity, the particularity, of God's dealings with the world. Revelation does not need to be construed as something absolutely universal, completely general, but as having a distinct form, determinate contours, a concrete shape. What is interesting is that with this emphasis on particularity comes not, as one might suppose, a narrowing of theology, but a quite dramatic broadening. If the issue is the perception of beauty rather than the testing, defending, or expounding of truth, then anything which reflects, mediates, and helps us to perceive the beauty becomes legitimate theological material. One of the most significant aspects of Balthasar's work is undoubtedly the way it opens up the playing field of theology, making reflection on the saints or on literary works not just a pious ornament or supplement to a proper theology, but central to the theological enterprise itself.

Something much lamented in recent theology is a divide between theology and spirituality, or between the theological and the mystical, or between theology and prayer. Balthasar's aesthetic approach, with this image of "seeing the form" at its center, finally, can lay some claim to overcoming this divide. Faith, as Balthasar presents it, is intrinsically contemplative; it has to do, not with accepting as true certain unverifiable propositions, but rather with seeing something, with grasping it as a totality, and with being transfixed by it. And if the whole of *The Glory of the Lord* is, directly or indirectly, focused around the beauty of the form, then it is has built into it throughout a contemplative dimension — or at the very least it is throughout ordered to contemplation.

There is a great deal, then, it seems, to be said for the theological program that arises out of this image of "seeing the form." It does something to meet the concerns of both a Barth and a Rahner while escaping the difficulties that can face their respective positions: to provide a way of articulating a critique of historical critical methods; to allow for a real opening up of the range and methods of theology; and to transcend the typical modern split between theology and spirituality.

Might there, however, be dangers in such a program? At the very least, it seems, certain *possible* dangers are associated with the image of "seeing the form," with placing this model of an aesthetic experience at the center of a major theological endeavor — dangers that arise from what one might call its all-or-nothing quality. Balthasar, we have seen, lays great emphasis on the *wholeness* of the form: one cannot see the form of revelation bit-by-bit, but only as a totality. Clearly, then, his project, particularly in its culminating discussion of the New Testament in Volume 7, not only is as a matter of fact but *has to be* ambitious. He cannot aim to illuminate some aspects of revelation, but must attempt to weave the New Testament together as a whole to bring out its beauty, its glory, the form of revelation as such. And if there is an all-or-nothing character to what is attempted, there must also, it would seem, be an all-or-nothing character to the reader's response. One sees the form, as Balthasar presents it, or one fails to do so. It is an approach, one could argue, which seems to envisage little room for disagreement, or even for limiting and qualifying one's agreement. It is an approach that seems to allow for the possibility of an author to stand above his reader: the author, who has already "seen the form," who is already in possession, as it were, of this central aesthetic experience — an experience relating not to some particular insight or set of insights but quite simply revelation as a whole — does what he can to indicate this central beauty to the readers, who in turn themselves either see or fail to see.[23]

Clearly one does not *have* to read the project in this way. To avoid such a reading one might on the one hand lay stress on Balthasar's comments on the infinite nature of this particular form, and on the impossibility of mastering it, and on the other emphasize the enormous effort Balthasar puts into examining the work of other thinkers — theologians, literary figures, saints. One might argue, then, that the proper way to understand Balthasar is not to suppose that he himself has once and for all

23. One way in which one might defend against such a charge is by insisting that it is never on Balthasar's account a question of possessing anything — that what is central to his thought is never grasping the whole, but rather being grasped by it. Such an emphasis on passivity and receptivity, on our being seized, transported, transformed, is indeed very much present in Balthasar. On its own, however, it does not much help with the difficulty under consideration. The more a theologian insists on his own passivity with respect to his subject matter, the more, it would seem, he eliminates the possibility of any *space* between his own thought and revelation, and so the less room will he leave for any probing and questioning of his position, and the less will he allow possibility for disagreement. Self-effacement passes here seamlessly, one might say, into something that looks rather like self-assertion.

seen a totality and definitively grasped its beauty, but that he is undertaking, and introducing his readers into, a continuous and strenuous effort to see more adequately, or to see again and anew, that whole which is dimly perceived. The *Theological Aesthetics* might be understood as one offering, one among many possible perhaps, one attempt to glimpse and say something about the glory of God given in revelation.

This more charitable reading is clearly a possibility. One might point to distinct passages which support it. In the first volume Balthasar writes that "the image of Christ cannot be fully 'taken in' as can a painting; its dimensions are objectively infinite, and no finite spirit can traverse them."[24] And in the final volume, with a loose reference to Philippians 3:12ff., Balthasar writes of pursuing the "one single thing that aims through all to express itself ... *but without fancying to ourselves that we have grasped it wholly.*"[25] And yet it is not possible entirely to banish the sense that with his use of the aesthetic analogy there always lurks the danger of an implication that not to accept Balthasar's theology is simply to fail to see, to lack the eyes of faith. For quite often what one meets in Balthasar's texts is not so much a sense of the progressive and never wholly successful struggle to perceive something that is too much for us, but of the rather simpler all-or-nothing logic surrounding the notion of seeing, and around the question of who can and who cannot "perceive the form."

At points this emerges quite explicitly. In an early discussion of beauty in the first volume of the *Glory of the Lord*, for instance, we read:

> Whoever insists that he can neither see [the primal phenomenon of beauty] nor read it, or whoever cannot accept it, but rather seeks to "break it up" critically into supposedly prior components, that person falls into the void.[26]

In more specifically theological contexts we regularly come across this same sense of a clear dividing line between those capable of perceiving

---

24. *Seeing the Form,* p. 512.

25. *The Glory of the Lord,* Volume 7: *Theology: The New Covenant,* trans. Brian McNeil, C.R.V. (San Francisco: Ignatius, 2003), p. 10 (emphasis added).

26. *Seeing the Form,* p. 20.

and those who are not. Consider the following passage, for instance, which follows upon the assertion that "All divine revelation is impregnated with an element of 'enthusiasm' (in the theological sense)":

> *Nothing can be done* for the person who cannot detect such an element in the Prophets and the "teachers of wisdom," in Paul and in John, to mention only these. *Nor can anything be done* for the person who persists in denying the fact that all of this quenches and more than fulfills the human longing for love and beauty, a longing which, previous to and outside the sphere of revelation, exhausted itself in impotent and distorted sketches of such a desperately needed and yet unimaginable fulfilment.[27]

Some people, it seems, simply fail to "see the form," to grasp what is there, and there is little more to be said about the matter. Or again, consider the contrast, and indeed opposition, between those who can perceive beauty and those who cannot which emerges in a discussion of the relation between the experience of natural beauty and the experience of the beauty of Christ: in both cases, insists Balthasar, those transported by beauty "must appear to the world to be fools, and the world will attempt to explain their state in terms of psychological or even physiological laws"[28] and in both cases, "one must have seen the same thing as they if one is to understand them."[29] Those who have not seen are not only sharply distinguished from those who have, but are said to be incapable of understanding the latter. In passages such as these, then, there is no sense whatsoever of anything like a continuum or gradation in the business of "seeing the form," no sense of an effort or a straining after a fuller seeing, but simply a division, a division which could not be sharper, between those who see and those who do not.

One can of course hear in this either-or which we meet so often in Balthasar's texts merely an echoing of the pattern of Johannine or Pauline thought. But is this all it is? It is hard not to wonder, especially in

27. Ibid., p. 123 (emphasis added).
28. Ibid., p. 33.
29. Ibid., p. 34.

light of what can frequently be a rather polemical tone and a somewhat sweeping dismissal of opponents, whether the logic of Balthasar's work here allows for any distinction between resistance to his own theological position and resistance to the gospel as such.

The Play

If the image of the person enraptured by a work of art is at the heart of *The Glory of the Lord,* at the heart of the second part of Balthasar's major trilogy, *Theo-Drama,* is the image of a play.

There is some precedent for taking drama as a metaphor for life, or indeed for history ("All the world's a stage . . .").[30] Balthasar's project involves a self-conscious and elaborate examination of the possibilities of this metaphor, together with a shift in its focus: the play in his account offers a framework, and a set of resources, for thinking, not only of the whole of history, but of the whole of history in relation to God, and God in relation to history. The "relation" here is a serious one: it is not just a question of a God who sits outside of everything, as a kind of ultimate spectator of the drama, or as the one who constructed the original stage. In fact, as Balthasar presents it, history is a play in which God is the author, the director, and also the chief actor (theses are the roles, respectively, of Father, Spirit, and Son). Furthermore, Balthasar suggests, God is himself, even apart from history, to be conceived through theatrical analogies: the eternal relations of the persons of the immanent Trinity are fundamentally dramatic, and, rather dizzyingly, Balthasar proposes that all of history can be thought of along the lines of a "play within a play."[31] History, as we ordinarily understand it, that is to say, is a drama which takes place in the space opened up by the more fundamental drama played out among the persons of the Trinity.

At first glance it is a rather startling move to cast nearly all of systematic theology (the second part of Balthasar's trilogy includes major

30. Balthasar in fact devotes over 120 pages to an examination of these precedents: cf. "The Idea of the World Stage" in the first volume of the *Theo-Drama.*

31. See *Theo-Drama: Theological Dramatic Theory,* Volume 1: *Prolegomena,* trans. Graham Harrison (San Francisco: Ignatius, 1983), p. 20.

treatments of Christology, theological anthropology, soteriology, escha-
tology, and the Trinity) in the framework of drama. Balthasar's approach
is undoubtedly novel, and opens up a significant range of new perspectives. But he would resist the idea that it as a merely arbitrary innova-
tion, on a number of grounds. First, one can trace a history of the interaction between Christianity and the theater, and, though the Church's
attitude to the theater has often been nervous or indeed negative, it is
possible to point to some significant borrowings by the Church from the
theater (the very language in which the doctrine of the Trinity is articulated, for instance), and also to a number of theologians who have, even
if only in a partial way, developed explicitly dramatic conceptions of
dogma.[32] Secondly, Balthasar presents his dramatic approach as something which brings together a whole range of tendencies or movements
in modern theology. He depicts eight themes of the theology of recent
decades, each of which has something to do with moving theology away
from "the sandbank of rationalist abstraction."[33] Each on his view is of
some value, but none alone "is adequate to provide the basis for a Christian theology." All of them, however, can find their fulfillment — indeed
their center — in the dramatic approach to theology, or so he believes.
He has tried to show, he writes, that "the substantial efforts of modern
theology are concentric, converging on a theo-drama, and that it is only
in relation to this center that they can reciprocally complement each
other."[34] He envisions his own approach, in other words, not as coming
from nowhere, but as that toward which modern theology has been,
without realizing it, pressing (and in which it finds its fulfillment). And finally, at the deepest level, it is central to Balthasar's self-understanding
as a theologian that he think of his project, not fundamentally as *invent-
ing* an interesting new way to present things, but as *responding* to what is
in fact given in revelation: "our view of God, the world and man will not
be developed primarily from below, out of man's understanding of him-

32. See *Theo-Drama: Theological Dramatic Theory,* Volume 2: *Dramatis Personae: Man
in God,* trans. Graham Harrison (San Francisco: Ignatius, 1990), pp. 152-69.

33. Balthasar presents these tendencies in modern theology under nine headings:
"Event," "History," "Orthopraxy," "Dialogue," "Political Theology," "Futurism," "Function,"
"Role," and "Freedom and Evil." Cf. *Prolegomena,* pp. 25-50.

34. Ibid., p. 77.

self: it will be drawn from that drama which God has already 'staged' with the world and with man, in which we find ourselves players."[35] There is certainly some sense in which Balthasar's approach to dogmatics in the *Theo-Drama* is a very fresh one, but it is not, he would want to insist, one that appears out of nowhere.

I began by stressing the centrality of God to the drama Balthasar presents — with Christ the principal actor, and the inner-Trinitarian "play" framing the whole history — as a way of distinguishing his from more familiar conceptions of the world as a stage and history as drama. But it is equally important to stress that *we* too have a role, even if a secondary one, in the drama. That we can have such a role, that there is room for real human freedom, for a genuine response to God, is in fact a central concern for Balthasar, and one of the themes that he sees a dramatic approach as particularly adapted to bringing out.

Balthasar can be read here as concerned to correct the theology of Karl Barth.[36] That Barth's theology is Christocentric, that it always attempts to begin from and return to Christ, rather than being governed by a prior theory or a purportedly universal perspective, was something of which Balthasar approved. But in Barth's *Church Dogmatics,* according to Balthasar, this insistence on Christ is taken so far that no room is left for any genuine freedom and response on our part, no true significance for the actions of anyone other than Christ. We are, as it were, cut right out of the story. One of the things Balthasar is concerned to stress, then, in developing a dramatic approach to theology, is that no matter how central and decisive Christ is to the "play" as a whole, his role is not of a kind to put an *end* to all drama, but rather to open up a genuine space in which we can act. The roles we are offered are secondary, made possible only by Christ, but they are nevertheless real roles, and roles which we are free to enact or to resist. One of Balthasar's recurring themes, indeed, is that Christ causes an *intensification* of drama, a heightening of conflict and tension, and that the follower of Christ lives not in a world where everything is already accomplished and the struggle over, but rather in a situation where because of

35. Ibid., p. 9.

36. In this reading I am influenced by Stephen Wigley's work. See his *Karl Barth and Hans Urs von Balthasar: A Critical Engagement* (London and New York: T&T Clark, 2007).

Christ everything is all the more polarized — polarized between God and the forces antagonistic to God. And this has genuine implications for what the Christian must do, and for what she must suffer.

Drama is a rich and complex phenomenon, and it in fact suggests a whole raft of possible themes and resources for theological exploration. There is the question, already touched on above, of the author, the director, and the actor, and the relationships among them. There is the issue, which Balthasar does much with in both his Christology and his understanding of mission, of the "role" that the actor takes on, and the relationship between this role and the one who plays the role. There are questions of dramatic tension, already touched on, of the interplay between different characters, and indeed the relationship between the individual characters, with their particular freedom, and the plot, the larger movement, of the drama. There is the question of drama and necessity — a drama is not something that is (or should be) predictable in advance, but after the fact it carries a certain sense of inevitability.

To attempt to do justice to all of these themes would be, in effect, to attempt a summary of the five major volumes of the *Theo-Drama*. We will in fact return to some of these themes in later chapters. But one aspect of Balthasar's deployment of the language of drama that is particularly important for our purposes here is its methodological implication, for Balthasar suggests that there is a way of doing theology which is particularly consonant with drama, a distinctly dramatic "style" of theology capable of being contrasted with other styles.

In a good Hegelian fashion (and in this case also borrowing his terms from Hegel) Balthasar traces in the history of Christian thought an opposition between two kinds of theology, "lyric" and "epic," and proposes that opposition is transcended in a third, namely, a dramatic mode of theology. The difference between lyric and epic theology, as Balthasar presents it, is the difference between a second-person and a third-person theology, between "spirituality" and a more "objective" theology. In lyric theology God is addressed directly; this is theology in the mode of "edifying utterance in the bosom of the Church, from faith to faith,"[37] and involves "the internal motion of the devout subject, his emotion and sub-

---

37. *Dramatis Personae: Man in God,* p. 56.

mission."[38] In epic theology, the aim is to be as objective and precise as possible; God and Christ here become "He," something which theology is *about,* and inevitably there is a sense of distance, as the theologian seems to stand away from and over the material as a kind of judge. The separation between the epic and the lyric came, Balthasar thinks, quite early in Christianity. It is not easily overcome by councils, for instance, beginning and ending what is essentially an epic mode of theology with prayers, nor by a thinker like Anselm interrupting his theology with direct address to God.[39] The two cannot, taken in themselves, simply be spliced together; to overcome the opposition between these two modes of theology, one needs to go beyond them both. "We shall not," writes Balthasar, "get beyond the alternatives of 'lyrical' and 'epic', spirituality (prayer and personal involvement) and theology (the objective discussion of facts), so long as we fail to include the dramatic dimension of revelation, in which alone they can discover their unity."[40]

To understand what it means to do theology in a dramatic style, it is important to note that God's interaction with the world as Balthasar presents it is in some sense a drama without audience — or at least, a drama without any *uninvolved* audience, without spectators who simply sit and watch. "In this play," writes Balthasar, "all the spectators must eventually become fellow actors, whether they wish to or not."[41] The drama of God's dealings with the world is all-encompassing, sucking everything into itself, making impossible the notion of any place — or indeed any person or any thinking — *outside* the play. It is a drama which "has already drawn all truth and all objectivity into itself."[42] A dramatic theology, then, is a theology which operates in accord with this situation, a theology which positions itself *within* rather than above or outside the drama: "For theology is not an adjunct to the drama itself: if it understands itself correctly, it is an aspect of it and thus has an inner participation in the nature of the drama."[43]

38. Ibid., p. 55.
39. Ibid., p. 56.
40. Ibid., p. 57.
41. Ibid., p. 58.
42. Ibid.
43. Ibid., p. 151.

On the face of it, this advocacy of a dramatic approach to theology would seem to suggest that some of the criticisms and the worries I have been articulating about Balthasar's theology must be misplaced. For surely the insistence that theology is done in the midst of the action, that theology is always already involved, and that it cannot, as the epic theologian wishes to, stand outside and survey everything — surely all this amounts to a rejection on Balthasar's part of just those things for which I am criticizing him?

Perhaps. But before considering the matter resolved, there are two kinds of questions which need to be asked. The first has to do with the relation of theory and practice. Balthasar *advocates* a dramatic approach to theology — that much is very clear — but does he actually employ one?

There are points, I think, where the answer should be "yes" — points where Balthasar clearly does write theology in a "dramatic" mode — times at which he presents us with the theology of one who is caught up, in the midst of things, and who cannot claim to have read or to have a grasp of the whole script in advance. His treatment of universal salvation in *Dare We Hope "That All Men Be Saved"?*[44] is a clear case in point. The title of the work itself brings out the stance adopted: the approach is to ask what *we*, Christians who in this life stand under both grace and judgment, may legitimately *hope* for — not simply how things are or even what we can *know*. Balthasar forcefully criticizes those who seem to know too much in this sphere, and argues against any flattening out or synthesis of the biblical texts. The whole piece is an exercise in resisting the temptations of an "epic" stance which pretends to survey and reconcile and arrive at closure: the position for which Balthasar ultimately argues, and the *way* in which he argues, both take into account our (and his own) position within the drama of judgment and salvation. (For a more detailed treatment of *Dare We Hope "That All Men Be Saved"?* see the appendix to this chapter.)

One can, then, find examples of Balthasar pursuing theology in an undoubtedly "dramatic" manner. The question, however, is whether a work like *Dare We Hope?* represents the dominant way in which Bal-

44. San Francisco: Ignatius, 1988.

thasar proceeds, or whether it is more in the nature of an exception. That Balthasar's thought often has, in spite of its explicit advocacy of a dramatic mode of thought, quite a strong inclination towards the epic, is something that Ben Quash has argued with some care in *Theology and the Drama of History*. Quash, through a series of case studies in Balthasar's treatment of both literary and biblical texts, highlights tendencies to flatten characters and to fail to do justice to their individuality, to read more resolution and harmony into texts than can legitimately be found in them, and in general to read so strongly through the lens of larger themes as to simplify and distort the material at hand. Quash further suggests that Balthasar's consistent diagnosis of sin as pride, self-assertion, Prometheanism, and the consequent insistence on the need for obedience, indifference, and abandonment amounts itself to a kind of flattening and reduction of human freedom and of any real drama within Balthasar's *Theo-Drama*: "Marian self-abandonment . . . is made to advertise a sort of ecclesial resolution of the interaction of God and the creature, which reflects in turn von Balthsar's great desire to see a generalizable shape in the life of believers."[45]

Quash, then, points to particular themes in Balthasar, and particular interpretive practices, which are at odds with his own commitment to a dramatic approach. In a later chapter I will be making similar suggestions about Balthasar's treatment of the life of the immanent Trinity. But there is also another, and perhaps simpler, way to put the question of the relation of theory to practice. How "dramatic," in the sense we have been discussing, is the very proposal to read all of history, all of God's dealings with history, and indeed the inner life of God itself, *as* an all-encompassing drama? Where is one standing when one makes this claim? Is there a contradiction, that is to say, between *what* Balthasar is asserting, and the very act of asserting it? If there is no position "outside" the play, and if we in particular are always involved and drawn into it, always already involved in the action, always already playing a role, can we at the same time propose to see the shape of the whole, and be in a position to characterize it as one vast drama embedded inside an-

45. Ben Quash, *Theology and the Drama of History* (Cambridge: Cambridge University Press, 2005), p. 161.

other? Is Balthasar himself, in his very construal of the whole of everything as a drama, not taking the role of theater critic — and perhaps also a theorist of drama — rather than of an actor *within* the drama?[46]

Balthasar's introduction of aesthetic and dramatic categories into the heart of theology is undoubtedly one of his most significant contributions to the discipline. Something fresh and original comes into contemporary theology with his use of the images we have been examining, and it is something which the theological world has yet to fully absorb.

We have seen that it also, however, has its troubling side. Though he never draws attention to himself or to his own role as a theologian, Balthasar's programmatic deployment of these images in fact silently positions him quite distinctly in relation to his readers and his materials. So the way he uses the aesthetic image, with his emphasis on the wholeness of the form, and with the tendency to make very clear, sharp contrasts between those who can perceive it and those who cannot, seems to lead to a theology which allows little room for argument, little space for a reader to question and disagree. In fact it leads to a situation in which it is hard to know how one might distinguish between being unpersuaded by Balthasar and lacking "the eyes to see" — how differing from Balthasar, in other words, is different from the absence of faith. And Balthasar's use of the image of the drama, fascinating though it is, seems implicitly to locate him well above all that he speaks of, so that ultimately he is in a position to survey not only all of world history, but all of history in relation to God, and God's own inner life, and describe the whole to us as a single play.

Appendix: The Hope for Universal Salvation

As I suggested in the body of this chapter, a clear exception to the general trend towards the "epic" in Balthasar's theology is to be found in the

---

46. I think it might be argued that Karl Barth on the one hand, and liberation theologians such as Gustavo Gutiérrez and Jon Sobrino on the other, would qualify much more readily as "dramatic" than does Balthasar.

little work he wrote towards the end of his life, *Dare We Hope "That All Men Be Saved"?*[47]

Is there really a hell? Is anyone actually damned, or will God in the end save all? These are things that we simply cannot know, Balthasar insists. But there is a difference between knowledge and *hope*. The key question, then, is not whether we should affirm or deny universal salvation, but whether it is something for which we can legitimately hope. And to this his answer is a definitive "yes."

Balthasar begins with a contrast between two sets of biblical texts. On the one hand one finds statements which point to an eternal loss, and on the other hand texts which speak of God's will, and ability, to save all. So on the one side there is the fact that Jesus speaks of God's judgment as a trial with a twofold outcome; there are images of outer darkness, weeping and gnashing of teeth, gehenna, the worm that shall not die; there is the threat that the sin against the Holy Spirit will not be forgiven, and so on. On the other hand, there are the many texts which use the word "all": God desires all people to be saved, Jesus Christ gave himself as a ransom for all; "supplications, prayers, intercession, and thanksgiving" should be made for all; the grace of God has appeared for the salvation of all; God wills to reconcile to himself all things, whether on earth or in heaven; God has decided to unite all things in Christ; God does not wish that any should perish, but that all should reach repentance; and so on.

Central to Balthasar's argument is the insistence that we must allow these two series of texts to stand side by side, without forcing them into a synthesis. And we must do this because of our own position: "All of us who practice the Christian Faith . . . are *under* judgment. By no means are we above it, so that we might know its outcome in advance and could proceed from that knowledge to further speculation."[48] The connection between being *under* judgment (always in the text there is this emphasis on the preposition) and the impropriety of synthesis, of harmonization, is one that Balthasar makes repeatedly: "What we have here are two se-

47. The German title, *Was dürfen wir hoffen?* (originally published in 1986), is a little less awkward. In English this work has been brought out together with "A Short Discourse on Hell," which Balthasar wrote in response to attacks on the position he took in *Was dürfen wir hoffen?* I will draw on both here.

48. *Dare We Hope?*, p. 13.

ries of statements that, in the end, because we are *under* judgment, we neither can nor may bring into synthesis";[49] "It is not for man, who is *under* judgment, to construct syntheses here."[50]

What Balthasar is insisting on, then, is that while there may indeed be a perspective which is above, or beyond, judgment — the perspective of God, or the perspective of the eschaton — this is a point of view which *we* do not have, and one which we must not arrogate to ourselves. Balthasar takes his stand, then, against those who know too much in either direction — both those who know that hell will ultimately be empty, and those who know that it will be populated. He suggests that Karl Barth, in spite of protestations to the contrary, is in danger of falling into the first camp.[51] On the whole, however, he focuses much more on grappling with those in the second camp, those who think they know that hell is populated, perhaps even quite heavily populated.[52]

Balthasar argues against this position on a number of fronts. First of all, to be certain that hell is populated is to refuse to take really seriously those texts which speak in universal terms. In trying to synthesize the two sets of texts mentioned above, then, theologians in fact subordinate one to the other: because they *know* the outcome of the judgment threatened in the one array of texts, they quietly limit and redefine the "all" which is affirmed in the other.

There is a danger also, Balthasar suggests, following Hans-Jürgen Verweyen, that a conviction that some are damned undermines the possibility of Christian love: "just the slightest nagging thought of a final hell for others brings on moments in which human togetherness becomes especially difficult. . . . If there may, in fact, be people who are absolutely incorrigible, why, then, should not those who make my life on earth a hell perhaps also be of that sort?"[53]

49. Ibid., p. 22.

50. Ibid., p. 23.

51. Ibid., pp. 44-45.

52. Balthasar's greater interest in grappling with those who know that some or many are damned is not surprising, given that such salvation-pessimism, unlike universalism, has in fact been a mainstream position in the Western theological tradition since Augustine.

53. P. 78, quoting from Verweyen, *"Das Leben aller als äusserster Horizont der Christologie."*

The absolute rejection of the possibility of universal salvation is also not compatible with the nature of Christian prayer: Balthasar cites a whole series of liturgical prayers which, obedient to 1 Timothy 2:1 (whose author urges "supplications, prayers, intercessions and thanksgivings" to be made for everyone), are made on behalf of all and for the salvation of all. 1 Timothy 2:1 "could not be asked," Balthasar argues, if the Church "were not allowed to have at least the hope that prayers as widely directed as these are sensible and might be heard."[54]

An interesting suggestion Balthasar makes in his "Short Discourse on Hell" is that those who have been confident that hell is heavily populated have also always been confident that they themselves will not end up there: "It can be taken as a motif running through the history of theology that, whenever one fills hell with a *'massa damnata'* of sinners, one also, through some kind of conscious or unconscious trick (perhaps cautiously, and yet reassuredly), places oneself on the other side."[55]

Fundamentally, Balthasar presents the conviction that there is a *massa damnata* as something which has led to the contortion and distortion of Christian thought and piety. We should be clear "how outrageous it is to blunt God's triune will for salvation . . . by describing it as 'conditional' and calling absolute only that divine will in which God allows his total will for salvation to be thwarted by man."[56] The theologians have "fragmented God's will for salvation," a fragmenting which leads to the "truly tragic, if not grotesque, history" of the doctrine of double predestination.[57] He points to a sermon by John Henry Newman as an example of the distorted piety that ultimately results from this position: Newman is himself tortured by the thought of all those who move headlong towards their damnation, and presents Christ on the cross as having his heart broken by the contemplation of the same thing, so that Christ not only died for sinners, but died *from* his recognition of his inability to save them. "After this kind of theology of the Cross," writes Balthasar, "where is any room left for rejoicing?"[58] From a

54. *Dare We Hope?*, p. 35.
55. Ibid., p. 191.
56. Ibid., pp. 23-24.
57. Ibid., p. 24.
58. Ibid., p. 27.

position such as this, there "can only be a despairing squirm at the sight of the Cross."[59]

In some ways this little volume is typically Balthasarian. A certain polemical element can be heard in it. A vast number of voices are called upon, and huge swathes of tradition are rapidly surveyed. The chapter on the New Testament deals in typical fashion with an enormous range of distinct texts in a very short space: on a single page in fact one can find Balthasar referring to passages from two different chapters each of 1 Corinthians, Romans, Hebrews, and John.[60] And, as often in Balthasar's writing, the whole has a certain meandering quality.[61]

But if the argument is not laid out in an especially disciplined fashion, on another level *Dare We Hope?* is nevertheless quite focused: all its elements are designed to explore and defend the claim that universal salvation cannot be known but can and must be hoped for. It is a book with a distinct and very clear point.[62] And it is one in which Balthasar does not aim to stand above the theological fray, but very much within it. He clearly takes a position in opposition to others, clearly places himself on one side of a debate.

If this writing from the midst of the fray is one thing which gives *Dare We Hope?* a certain dramatic quality, the other is the way Balthasar is so consistent in maintaining that where we stand decisively shapes what we can say. We are in a particular position both with respect to God ("under" and not *above* judgment) and also in time (in this life and not the next, "under" and not *beyond* judgment). We must live with a tension

59. Ibid., p. 26.

60. *Dare We Hope?*, p. 34.

61. So, for instance, both Karl Rahner (with whom, in this context, Balthasar is in complete accord) and Karl Barth appear in the chapter entitled "The New Testament," and both Gabriel Marcel and again Rahner are given substantial coverage in the chapter entitled "Thomas Aquinas."

62. One mark of this unusually tight focus on the defense of a particular position is the "dog which did not bark," the absence of some of the themes which so often weave their way through Balthasar's writing, some of which we will be touching on in later chapters: one finds here no trace, for instance, of Balthasar's usual interest in gender and a gendered construal of divine, human, and divine-human relations, no trace of his usual emphasis on suffering and obedience as central to the Christian life, no trace of his frequent concern with the nature of intra-trinitarian relationships.

(the tension represented by the two distinct arrays of texts) which we cannot, from this position, resolve. And Balthasar really does refuse to resolve it. His theology in this case, then, remains true — far more, ironically, than in the *Theo-Drama* itself — to the claim that "there is no standpoint from which we could observe and portray events as if we were uninvolved narrators of an epic"[63] and so "no standpoint external to theo-drama."[64]

63. *Dramatis Personae: Man in God,* p. 58.
64. Ibid., p. 62.

CHAPTER 4

Central Images 2: Fulfillment and the Circle

In the previous chapter, we looked at images that very clearly sit at the heart, respectively, of two of Balthasar's vast works — images, that is, which Balthasar more or less explicitly foregrounds. In this chapter the focus will be on images and patterns of thought which are not so obviously central, but which recur widely across Balthasar's writings and are at least as important, if not more so, in coming to grips with the nature of his theology. The first of these is a pattern I shall call, for the sake of brevity, "fulfillment": a range of possibilities is surveyed, each of them determined to be inadequate, and a single solution offered which is presented, not only as succeeding where the others fail (or being fully adequate where the others are only partially so) but also as taking up and integrating into itself all that is positive in the others. Secondly, there is a very widely recurring image of what I shall term a "radiating circle": there is a central point, or an inner circle, out of which (or into which, depending on what exactly is at stake) radiate a series of lines.

What I am attempting in this chapter, it is important to be clear, is not an examination of recurring *themes* in Balthasar's thought. At issue is not just one notion of fulfillment in Balthasar's theology, nor one central idea which is conveyed by the radiating circle image: in both cases, a single pattern is found in varied contexts, and used in these differing contexts in different ways and for different purposes. But it will be the burden of this chapter to show that attention to these patterns can nevertheless illuminate both the style of Balthasar's thought and some of its dangers.

Fulfillment

What I am describing as a fulfillment pattern[1] in Balthasar's thinking involves the survey of a range of possibilities, the introduction of a "solution" which succeeds where all the others fail (or at least where all others do not *wholly* succeed), and which in some way absorbs or fulfills the others. Before attempting to say anything about the significance of this pattern, it will be helpful to look at some examples. I will outline five here, chosen somewhat arbitrarily but from varied contexts in Balthasar's thought.

We can begin with something already touched upon in the previous chapter — the relation of dramatic to epic and lyric theology. Initially Balthasar introduces the epic and lyric as, apparently, the two fundamental modes of Christian theology:

> At a very early stage . . . the river of Christian utterance splits into two streams: the lyrical, edifying utterance in the bosom of the Church, from faith to faith, and the epic mode used for "external" relations, that is, at councils and in the theological and polemical treatises dealing with heretics or the threat of error.[2]

Each of these is good and necessary, but also each is in some way inadequate. Lyric theology, which Balthasar aligns with spirituality, has a kind of authenticity, in that the reality of the individual's relation to God shapes the way theological language is used: "God and Christ are addressed as 'Thou.'"[3] Such theology is not, however, sufficient for all purposes. When it is a question of addressing "pagans and Jews and waver-

---

1. "Fulfillment" has quite distinct connotations in Christian theology: one may think of the fulfillment of prophecies, or of Christ as the fulfillment of the law, and so on. Here, however, as will soon become clear, I am using the word in a rather broad and loose way. I have deliberately avoided choosing a term which too explicitly invokes Hegel, such as *Aufhebung*, since I am wanting to retain a focus on Balthasar's pattern of thought considered in its own right, rather than engaging in a genealogical debate.

2. *Theo-Drama*, Volume 2: *The Dramatis Personae: Man in God*, trans. Graham Harrison (San Francisco: Ignatius, 1990), pp. 55-56.

3. Ibid., p. 56.

ing or wayward Christians,"[4] the lyric will not do, and theology moves into an epic mode, speaking "about" God — but such speaking is done, writes Balthasar, "perhaps with a certain regret or a kind of bad conscience."[5] This distinction between epic and lyric Balthasar presents as a kind of dilemma, a problem, and it is a problem to which the dramatic approach to theology is offered as solution: "We shall not get beyond the alternatives of 'lyrical' and 'epic', spirituality (prayer and personal involvement) and theology (the objective discussion of facts), so long as we fail to include the dramatic dimension of revelation, in which alone they can discover their unity."[6] The dramatic approach is not merely a third which sits alongside the epic and the lyric, then, but a resolution, which includes both,[7] while overcoming the tension between them.

For a second example, we turn to a passage located quite late in the first volume of *The Glory of the Lord,* in which Balthasar undertakes a very brief placement of Christ among the world religions. In a matter of five pages, Balthasar contrasts Christ with all other religious founders, on a number of grounds: all others point to a way, Jesus "presents *himself* as the way";[8] all others have a moment of conversion, discovery, enlightenment, whereas Jesus is from the beginning the Son of the Father; in other religions salvation is either denial of the world or its reaffirmation,[9] in Christ alone "the structure of 'the present aeon' has been gripped in the vice of history and lifted from its hinges."[10] And so only in Christ can "this either/or of negation and transfiguration" be overcome: all the other religious founders "are caught up in the dialectic between God and the world, between the One and what is other," while Christ's revelation of the Trinity introduces something wholly new and avoids all

---

4. Ibid., p. 55.

5. Ibid., p. 56.

6. Ibid., p. 57.

7. Thus, for instance, "the epic is not abolished by the dramatic but incorporated into it" (p. 59).

8. *Glory of the Lord,* Volume 1: *Seeing the Form,* trans. Erasmo Leiva-Merikakis (Edinburgh: T&T Clark, 1982), p. 502.

9. One finds "cosmic myths and mythical systems which fundamentally could only choose either to negate the Being of the world as such for the sake of the divine Being . . . or to make visible anew . . . the primal divine law that permeates the world's Being" (ibid., p. 505).

10. Ibid., p. 505.

that is unsatisfactory in the others;[11] and so on. The general principle is that Christ stands apart as unique, but at the same time "he fulfils the partial truths contained in the religious myths of all peoples."[12]

Our third example recurs at a number of points. In various passages one can find Balthasar presenting oriental religion on the one hand, and Marxism on the other, as the two fundamental options offered by the modern world. The two are typically set in opposition to each other — one oriented towards contemplation and the other towards action, one primarily personal and the other social, one representing the "pagan," the other Judaism[13] — and then Christianity presented as that which differs from but fulfills them both. In one of his retrospective pieces, for instance, after introducing Marxism and "oriental (pagan) religiosity" and then setting the Christian proclamation over against them, Balthasar writes, "And so the personal is brought back to itself by the social and *vice versa,* so that the Christian dramatic shows itself to be, as it were by its very nature, at the centre between, and raised above, the two fundamental attempts to give meaning to the world and to existence, attempts that are possible when you start with the world itself."[14]

With our fourth example we return to the sphere of internal differentiation within Christian theology. In a section entitled "Delineating the form of faith" in the first volume of *The Glory of the Lord,* Balthasar sets out two contrasting ways of approaching Christian revelation. The first, the way of the neo-scholastics,[15] involves treating revelation as a series

11. Ibid., p. 506.

12. Ibid., p. 496.

13. Balthasar regularly presents Marxism as fundamentally "Judaic" or as "Neo-judaism," without necessarily giving a full explanation.

14. See "Another Ten Years," in *My Work: In Retrospect,* trans. by various hands (San Francisco: Ignatius, 1993), p. 100. Cf. *Truth Is Symphonic: Aspects of Christian Pluralism,* trans. Graham Harrison (San Francisco: Ignatius, 1987), pp. 180ff., for a contrast between Buddhism and "Neo-Judaism" more generally, and *A Short Primer for Unsettled Laymen,* trans. Mary Theresilde Skerry (San Francisco: Ignatius, 1985), for the suggestion that "the whole timeliness of Christianity today" should be able to be seen "in the elementary fact that *it alone* in the history of the world is *the superior unity of paganism and Judaism,* then as today" (p. 24, emphasis added).

15. More specifically, Balthasar attributes it to "the Baroque scholasticism and Neo-Scholasticism of the Jesuits."

of historical signs, signs which are sufficiently credible to persuade reason, and which point beyond themselves to invisible mystery. The second way, which Balthasar attributes to a wide array of figures (the Alexandrians, Augustine, Thomas Aquinas, Blondel, Scheuer, Marechal, Rousselot), puts more emphasis on the luminous nature of Being, the mind's dynamism towards it, and the light of faith. Each of these approaches has its weaknesses. In the first, with its insistence on signs which are rationally discernible, "the divine witness becomes one (exceptional) case among others; the divine quality does not leap into prominence, neither on the side of insight or vision nor on the side of faith."[16] In the second, there is the question of whether justice is done to the objective side of Christianity, and also "whether this whole orientation is not constantly threatened by a secret and, occasionally, even by an open bondage to philosophy which makes the internal standard of the striving spirit . . . to be somehow the measure of revelation itself."[17] Each of the two ways, Balthasar tells us, "grasps but one side of Christian faith, and of the insight and vision which belongs to it," and so, not too surprisingly, he asserts that "these two tendencies ought to be brought together."[18] The aesthetic approach to theology, with the centrality of the category of beauty, is then introduced and, implicitly at least,[19] presented as that which *does* in fact bring the two together.

Our final example is drawn from the opening chapters of *Love Alone: The Way of Revelation*.[20] In the first chapter, Balthasar discusses the "cos-

16. *Seeing the Form*, p. 148.

17. Ibid., p. 149.

18. Ibid., p. 150.

19. In this case the "fulfillment," while strongly indicated, is not quite explicit, because the argument takes an extra turn. Balthasar writes that the two tendencies in Christian theology can only be brought together if "they are purged of a common deficiency" (p. 150), namely, the tendency to see historical facts as pointing to something beyond themselves, to set up a dualism between "ostensive sign and signified interior light" (p. 151). Strictly speaking, Balthasar introduces the aesthetic approach here only as the means of overcoming this latter dualism — but it is hard to make sense of the general direction of the passage if one does not presume that it is therefore also the approach which can bring together the two tendencies in theology which have been under consideration.

20. Trans. Alexander Dru (London: Sheed and Ward, 1968).

mological method" in theology[21] — the approach, as he presents it, of the patristic period, the Middle Ages, and the Renaissance, in which Christianity is confidently envisaged as the unification, purification, and fulfillment of all that is to be found in philosophy and the religions: "All the unifying principles of the ancient world — such as the Logos of the stoics, the Neo-Platonic hierarchy of being rising from matter to the supra-essential One, the abstract majesty of the unifying power of Rome — all these were regarded as baptizable anticipations of the God-Logos in person who entered Israelite history, filled the whole world, in whom were the Ideas which were the pattern by which the world was made, and in relation to whom the world could be understood." In the second chapter, he then turns to the "Anthropological method" of the modern period, a method in which "the attempt was made to transfer the locus of verification from a cosmos becoming more and more godless (and so having less and less in common with Christianity) to man as the epitome of the world."[22] And the fundamental thesis of these opening chapters is that neither of these approaches will do. So we read, for instance, that "Christian self-understanding (and so theology) is found neither in a wisdom superior to that of the world's religions, based on divine information . . . nor on the definitive fulfillment of man as a personal and social being through the realization of the effects of a revelation and redemption." Or again that "If the first approach [the cosmological] suffers the limitations of a past age, this second [the anthropological] is methodologically in error: the framework of God's message to man in Christ cannot be tied to the world in general, nor to man in particular." At the end of the second chapter, the question of "where next" is then posed: "For if God's sign cannot be verified either by reference to the world or by reference to men — then how is it to be done?"[23] And finally in Chapter 3,

21. There is a certain ambiguity in *Love Alone* as regards what fundamentally is being examined and commended. Quite often the issue seems to be apologetics, the business of laying "the credibility of the Christian message before the world in the most favorable light" (p. 11). But at times Balthasar's language indicates that something more general is at stake; in the preface, for instance, as we shall consider below, he indicates that the aim is to demonstrate that "this theological approach [theological aesthetics] . . . is in fact the one possible approach to the heart of theology" (p. 8).

22. *Love Alone*, pp. 12-13, 25.

23. Ibid., p. 41.

then, the "third way," the "way of love" is presented, a combination of an "aesthetic" and a personalist approach. One might suppose that since the first and second chapters represent different periods, Balthasar sees himself simply as posing a new and more appropriate approach for our own period (one which might logically at some stage be surpassed by something else again). But in fact it is clear that he sees himself as doing something more than just presenting the next on the list, offering a third method for a third period which is otherwise on an equal footing with the others. In the preface, for instance, Balthasar describes himself as trying to show "that this theological approach, far from being a dispensable theological by-road, is in fact the one possible approach to the heart of theology — the cosmic world-historical approach, and the path of anthropological verification, being secondary aspects, complementary to it."[24] Having surveyed the available possibilities, in other words, and seen them each to be in some way lacking, Balthasar is not only proposing the solution, but presenting it as overarching, and taking up into itself, or at least placing in relation to itself, the other available options.

All this is a very rapid tour through a great deal of material — too rapid, naturally, to allow for any kind of assessment of the concrete claims made in each case. What is of interest for the moment, however, is not the particular positions Balthasar is taking, but the presence of the common pattern of thought in these varied contexts. As we have already suggested, in each of these cases, there is a survey of a range of possibilities, whether this be possible worldviews, possible ways of doing theology, or possible ways of thinking about revelation. In many cases, though not always, the range of possible positions is in fact a range of only *two* positions, which then tend to be set up as in some way opposites. In each example, the various possibilities that are introduced are deemed to be inadequate, or at least less than fully adequate. Thus lyric theology is insufficiently exact and objective for many purposes, but epic improperly seems to stand as judge over its material; the cosmological approach is wedded to a no longer tenable view of the world, but the anthropological is "methodologically flawed," and so on. At times, when only two possibilities are surveyed, not only the particular weaknesses of each, but also

24. Ibid., 8-9.

the opposition between the two is presented as calling for some kind of resolution (this is particularly clear in the first and fourth of our examples). And in each case a resolution is introduced — one further possibility, to which attach none of the flaws found in the others, but which itself can in some way incorporate, include, or unify what was good and necessary in the less than fully successful possibilities.

One further point is worth noting in this pattern. Balthasar never gives the impression of offering just *some* alternative views against which to consider his preferred position. In each case, that is to say, the possibilities examined are framed, not as *a* range of possibilities, but rather as *the* range of possibilities. Epic, lyric, and dramatic appear as *the* possible modes of Christian theology. Balthasar does not contrast Christ just with some other founder of a religion, or some particular selection of founders: he gives an account of Christ in relation to *all* religious founders. Marxism and oriental mysticism are not just two other worldviews: they, together with Christianity, are the *only* worldviews which are a real possibility in the contemporary world. And so on.

I have emphasized that what is under consideration here is not a single theological point that Balthasar makes repeatedly in different ways, but a range of positions *patterned* in the same way. It is time now, however, to allow the analysis to become a little more complex, for it would be misleading to discuss this pattern without acknowledging that "fulfillment" is *also,* in Balthasar's thought, a distinct, in fact quite central, theological theme. Indeed, some of the examples of the fulfillment pattern of thought I have sketched are *also* examples of Balthasar's commitment to this theme. The fulfillment pattern, in other words, shows itself, *among other places,* when he is working out the fulfillment theme.

As a *pattern,* as I have described it, fulfillment might in principle characterize an argument about any subject whatsoever. I might survey all the main theories of the causes of the French revolution, present them all as inadequate, and then introduce my own theory as that which escapes the weaknesses of all the others while unifying within itself all that is of value in the rest, achieving what they all strove for. To speak of a distinctly theological *theme* of fulfillment in Balthasar, on the other hand, is to indicate something about the way he relates Christ and Christianity to all that lies, or seems to lie, outside of it. Balthasar has no desire to paint that which lies beyond the bounds of Christianity as totally wrong, or simply the result of sin, or completely without worth. It will, of course, have elements of falsity and sin, on his account, but the most fundamental way in which Balthasar presents the non-Christian is as *partial* — containing positive elements which it cannot bring into a whole, striving for something that it cannot attain, possessing fragmentary elements of truth and goodness but incapable in its own terms of reaching beyond the fragmentary. His way of relating Christ and Christianity to the non-Christian, then, is not fundamentally as a negation (as one might find in the Barth of *Romans*), nor fundamentally as the making explicit of that which was implicit (as one might find in the Rahner of *Foundations of Christian Faith*), but as the (unexpected and unanticipatable) fulfilling of that which was present but in a confused and partial way.[25]

In some cases the fulfillment *pattern* in Balthasar's thinking, then, is closely connected to his vision of Christ as the fulfillment of all religions, cultures, and philosophies, and so his use of the pattern can be explained by his commitment to the vision. But this cannot be true in every case, for a fulfillment pattern is at work in Balthasar's thought, as we have seen, not only when he relates Christ or Christianity to that which is other to it, but also when, already within the sphere of Christianity, he relates one (preferred) kind of theology to others — thus, in the examples we have sketched, epic fulfills the dramatic and lyric, and a theological aesthetics fulfills both the extrinsicist and illuminations approaches to revelation on the one hand, and the cosmological and anthropological methods in theology on the other.

An unfriendly way to read Balthasar would be to suppose that in fact there *is* continuity between these different instances of fulfillment. Just

25. Balthasar's *Epilogue,* trans. Edward T. Oakes, S.J. (San Francisco: Ignatius, 2004), written after his trilogy to "afford the weary reader something like an overview of the whole enterprise" (p. 9), opens with a chapter entitled "Integration as Method," which sets out relatively clearly, and in the space of four short pages, Balthasar's vision of the partial truth contained in non-Christian worldviews and an apologetic method which involves demonstrating how all these partial truths can be integrated into higher levels of vision and ultimately shown to point, in their partial but incomplete truth, towards the higher resolution found in Christian revelation.

as Balthasar sees Christianity as the fulfillment of all other religions and worldviews, so, it might be suggested, he is inclined to see his own theology (whether in its aesthetic or dramatic phase) as the fulfillment of all other theological tendencies within the tradition. On such an unfriendly reading one might say that he is placing himself, within the Christian theological tradition, in a position analogous to that which he gives to Christ within the world — that he is placing the tradition within which he stands as the fulfillment of all other traditions, and his own thought as the fulfillment of this tradition.

But it is surely not necessary to read Balthasar in this way. One can see the various instances of the fulfillment pattern, not as interlocking pieces of a grand scheme, but as the expression of a certain habit of thought, a tendency to see and to present material in a particular way, to think according to a certain pattern. What must still be noted, however, is just how ambitious the kind of thinking associated with this pattern is. Balthasar is regularly presuming that he is in a position to survey a totality (*all* of world religions, *all* of the worldviews which represent serious options for the contemporary person, *all* of the manners of doing theology, and so on), to diagnose the inadequacies and limitations of each of the elements (or of all but one of the elements) in this totality, and then to place all these elements with respect to, and to relate them to, the one "fulfillment."

In Balthasar's defense here two points might be made. The first is that in some of the cases in question — those where it is a matter of relating Christ or Christianity to other figures or worldviews — what is on display is not any particular level of ambition or confidence Balthasar has in his *own* thought, but a very high view of *Christ*. The suggestion that it is intellectually overambitious to propose Christ as the fulfillment of all religion, myth, philosophy, and even all world-views, then, is just mistaken — or at the very least it would amount to a rather high-handed and *a priori* ruling out of court of a particular Christological commitment. And it might be argued, secondly, that in other cases — those "fulfillment" patterns where Balthasar is writing about different possibilities *within* Christian theology — he is really doing no more than what almost any scholar does in the course of her writing. For surely one does not propose a new theory or a new approach without taking note of, and both learning from and being dissatisfied with, that which has gone before. And so, presumably, a large proportion of all scholarship amounts in some way to proposing a new theory, or approach as superior to others, while at the same time taking into account what was valuable in their efforts. In short, a defender might say that Balthasar is being somehow blamed here for what amounts to nothing but high Christology on the one hand, and normal scholarly practice on the other.

However, the sense that an unusual level of ambition is present in this recurring fulfillment pattern, a quite striking presumption to survey and command vast arrays of territory, cannot be laid to rest quite so easily. A distinction needs to be drawn, first of all, between positing Christ as the fulfillment of all religion, culture, philosophy, and so on, and actually presuming the capacity to survey and describe *how* Christ is such a fulfillment. That Christ must be the fulfillment of all culture philosophy and religion might, on certain accounts, be a matter of faith, a position that follows from one's understanding of Jesus Christ and his relation to creation, from one's understanding of nature and grace, and so on — and this is certainly the case for Balthasar. But it is another matter to suppose that one is actually in a position to *see* how all things in their fragmentariness point to and find unanticipated fulfillment in Christ, to see how in fact the pattern fits together. To put it at its simplest, to suppose that all things must be related to Christ is one thing, but to suppose that one can know the relation of all things to Christ is quite a different thing. In his defense, I suggested above, perhaps it could be said that Balthasar was exhibiting a high view of Christ rather than a high confidence in his own thought, but in fact we find the two very closely united: the strong sense that Balthasar has of Christ as fulfillment of all things seems matched by an equally strong sense of his own capacity to see and describe this universal fulfilling.[26]

26. It is quite striking, in this connection, that while Balthasar prefaces the extremely broadly ranging *Glory of the Lord* with something of an apology, it is an apology not for its breadth but for its *narrowness:* the scope of the work "remains all too Mediterranean" and the limitations of his education have prevented him from extending his reach to Asian cultures. Indeed, in later writings he seems to want to make good these deficiencies. In the *Epilogue,* for instance, Balthasar extends his reach to include (however briefly) not only Islam, but Shintoism, Taoism, Confucianism, Zen, Mahayana Buddhism, and forms of Hinduism.

But can Balthasar's use of the fulfillment pattern in general be seen simply as a version of the normal scholarly practice of presenting one's own proposal against a background of previous positions? Two things militate against this. One is the tendency, already noted, not so much to set his preferred approach off against *some* alternative positions, but rather to present something much closer to an account of *all* possible approaches or solutions before introducing the one which alone is adequate and which takes up into itself or integrates all others. The second is the sheer variety and scope of the claims Balthasar makes: to survey all worldviews which are possible for us; to relate and contrast Christ with all other religious founders, and the doctrine of the Trinity with all other approaches to the one and the many; to depict all possible modes of theological utterance, all the fundamental ways of reading revelation, all the basic methods in theology.

With this recurring appearance of the fulfillment pattern, then, what we seem to find is repeated occasions on which Balthasar serenely stands above his material, surveying it in its totality, explaining to us how it all fits together. Of course it is possible to say that there is ultimately nothing improper here. Balthasar's is, after all, a towering intellect, he is after all "perhaps the most cultivated man of his time," and perhaps we must accept that towering intellects simply *do* rise above things and achieve, repeatedly, great overviews.

In any case, this theme of the "overview" is one with which we will continue to wrestle in our next section. And if the manner in which we have thus far seen Balthasar standing above and surveying his material might possibly be defensible, in what is to be examined next this same tendency becomes, as we shall see, distinctly more problematic.

The Radiating Circle

The radiating circle is an image in Balthasar's thought which might easily be overlooked; it is not centrally foregrounded in any one work, nor does it have the Hegelian resonance which makes the fulfillment pattern stand out so distinctly. But the radiating circle is an image which in fact is both frequent and very widely diffused in Balthasar's writing.

Imagine a circle, then, with lines coming out of it — or going into it — rather like the sun, as drawn by a child. The central circle (sometimes it is just a single point) is special in some way that the radiating lines are not, but on the other hand the lines are accessible or describable in some way that the circle (or central point) is not. This is a pattern which one comes across with considerable regularity in Balthasar's writings.

Let us begin, again, simply with a few examples. In a discussion of the nature of "office" in the Church, Balthasar writes:

> It is thus possible that interpretations varying according to the time and the particular emphases may yet meet at the center, just as different transverse sections of an object may all pass through the center. They will be consistent with one another only insofar as they actually make contact with the center and radiate forth from it, and insofar as, despite their external differences, they are ultimately in affinity.[27]

In the final volume of *The Glory of the Lord,* in a discussion of the relation of various Old Testament motifs to the theology of the cross, we read:

> These hints are to be considered seriously; they have enough power to encircle the mystery of the Cross in such a way that the lines coming from the Old Testament genuinely intersect each other in the midpoint of this mystery. . . . Earliest Christian faith . . . sought to interpret the Cross as the point of unity of the converging lines of power, while at the same time showing its transcendence that makes the Cross the starting-point of a new Christian reflection that can never be finished, because here "unsearchable riches" (Eph. 3:8) lie "hidden" (Col. 2:3).[28]

In the context of asserting that a continuous history of theological aesthetics does not exist, he tells us:

---

27. *Explorations in Theology,* Volume 2: *Spouse of the Word,* trans. A. V. Littledale, with Alexander Dru (San Francisco: Ignatius, 1993), p. 127.

28. *Glory of the Lord,* Volume 7: *Theology: The New Covenant,* trans. Brian McNeil, C.R.V. (San Francisco: Ignatius, 2003), p. 203.

In the new constellations of intellectual history there break out from time to time from the midpoint which is beyond history new and original perceptions. . . . Each original form breaks out anew from the centre.[29]

In a general discussion of methodology in Christology in the third volume of the *Theo-Drama* we read:

There has to be a plurality of New Testament theologies: only thus can they give an idea of the transcendence of the one they proclaim. So much so that it confirms our a priori expectation that even an individual speaker — like Paul — can operate from different perspectives and so, by means of different accents, concepts and symbols, point toward the transcendent central phenomenon.[30]

After expressing a worry, in *Love Alone,* that modern theological enthusiasms are in danger of obscuring the heart of the gospel, Balthasar turns for contrast to pre-modern theology:

The cosmological and anthropological deductions drawn by the Fathers of the Church and the great spiritual teachers are disposed round that centre as though in the form of a monstrance designed to hold up the eucharistic heart to our view. They are simply functions of that one centre, and lose their significance in providing a perspective of the world the moment the scandal of the Cross is blurred in the slightest degree.[31]

And finally, in introducing the set of short essays that make up *Elucidations,* he writes:

---

29. *Glory of the Lord,* Volume 2: *Studies in Theological Styles: Clerical Styles,* trans. Andrew Louth, Francis McDonagh, and Brian McNeil, C.R.V. (Edinburgh: T&T Clark, 1984), p. 20.

30. *Theo-Drama,* Volume 3: *Dramatis Personae: Persons in Christ,* trans. Graham Harrison (San Francisco: Ignatius, 1992), p. 144.

31. *Love Alone,* p. 123.

Together they [a set of essays] bear witness to an underlying view of things; they are a few rays which all radiate from the same centre....

If these few rays do proceed from the true sun, then perhaps one could on that basis calculate the centre of the fire from which our questions would be shown to be truly burning.[32]

The list of examples could readily be extended. The range of contexts in which the image is deployed is, as the examples indicate, broad. We find it at work in relating multiple Old Testament themes to Christ, manifold New Testament theologies to that which unifies them, and a multiplicity of perspectives throughout the tradition to the one revelation; we also find it when Balthasar wants to discuss the many themes or concerns of a particular author in relation to a single interest or inspiration, when he describes how the many strands of modern theology stand in relation to his own proposed theo-dramatic theory, and even, indeed, when he writes of how a variety of sayings of Christ relate to a single attitude.

There are, it must be acknowledged, certain variations in the pattern: in some cases the emphasis is on lines moving *out from* the center, in others it is on movement *towards* the central point; sometimes an intersection of lines is indicated, at others only a convergence; sometimes all the elements of the image are explicitly articulated, at others the pattern is only sketchily indicated through a reference to a convergence of many different things on a single one.

In a number of instances the image of the radiating circle is found conjoined with a rejection of the possibility of systematizing: we are told either that that which is at the center cannot be defined and tied down into a system, or else that the multiplicity of rays cannot themselves be systematized and tidily related to each other, for they can be properly understood in relation to each other only if seen in their common relation to the one center. In almost every case, furthermore, there is the suggestion that that which is at the center is in some way mysterious: at times it is explicitly termed a mystery, at others it is characterized as transcendent, or outside history, or undefinable, or invisible. Interestingly, this seems to be true even when the radiating circle imagery is de-

---

32. *Elucidations,* trans. John Riches (San Francisco: Ignatius, 1998), p. 7.

ployed to characterize Balthasar's *own* work. In the preface to the first volume of *Explorations in Theology,* for instance, Balthasar acknowledges that in the sketches to follow, certain things will be "approached and studied from many angles," and suggests that this is to be attributed "to the fascination generated by the unseen core of the subject matter."[33] And if this seems to portray Balthasar himself as circling around something mysterious, in another context we find, as we have already seen, the suggestion that all or most of the major streams of twentieth-century theology in fact circle around and converge on his own theo-dramatic approach, which is then itself given a certain mysterious character. This is perhaps most clearly stated in the second volume of the *Theo-Drama:* looking back on what he had said in the first with regard to nine tendencies in modern theology, Balthasar writes, "at the time we observed that they converged and pressed toward a theo-dramatic context but could not reach it," and then goes on to suggest that there is something intrinsically elusive about theo-drama — "Since the all-embracing context cannot fall under any general concept, theo-drama cannot be defined: it can only be approached from various angles."[34]

If the radiating circle is frequently in Balthasar's writing associated with a rejection of system, and even more frequently to be found in connection with a reference to mystery, it is, in *every* case, fundamentally a way of dealing with pluralism, a way of coherently ordering a multiplicity, whether this is a multiplicity of Old Testament motifs, or New Testament writings, or of sayings of Christ, or of theologies of the Cross, or of conceptions of the Christian life, of theological styles in the Tradition, or of modern approaches to theology, or of Balthasar's own essays.

33. *Explorations in Theology,* Volume 1: *The Word Made Flesh,* trans. A. V. Littledale, with Alexander Dru (San Francisco: Ignatius, 1989), p. 7.

34. *The Dramatis Personae: Man in God,* p. 62. Interestingly, it would have been possible to include this example — the way Balthasar here relates other modern theological movements to his own proposal of theo-drama — in the previous section, because essentially he is suggesting that his theodramatic approach *fulfills* all these major twentieth-century trends, going beyond them all but taking up into itself what is positive in them. There is, then, a certain overlap between the two thought patterns we are discussing here: the way in which the "lines" from the Old Testament intersect in Christ, who nevertheless transcends them, is another example. But there is certainly not a complete coincidence: most of the radiating circle images do not fall into a fulfillment pattern, at least not immediately.

The characteristic way in which Balthasar relates these three elements — the rejection of system, the reference to mystery, and the ordering of a multiplicity — can be seen in his discussion of the meaning of the Cross:

> What takes place in the "hour" remains a mystery and can never be reduced to a "system" — even in the interpretations attempted by the primitive Church. So there is nothing strange about the fact that the Passion narratives, and subsequently the theological interpretations of the Cross, employ different theologoumena, circling concentrically around a transcendent core.[35]

We have, here, a multiplicity — more than one Passion narrative, more than one theological interpretation of the Cross — and the multiplicity is ordered through its relation to a center ("circling concentrically around a transcendent core"). That there is this multiplicity is not to be construed as a problem, but as the corollary of the transcendent — perhaps one could say the transcendently meaningful — character, of what lies at the center: the multiplicity of interpretations follows from and confirms the mysterious character of "the hour." Both "mystery" and the transcendence of what lies at the center are then in contrast with the notion of "system": if one could produce a system to explain the significance of the Cross once and for all, if one could reduce it to a limited number of logically and tidily ordered statements, it would become something within our control, its transcendent character lost.

We have, then, a frequently recurring image or pattern of thought, often found in the vicinity of a rejection of systematizing theology and an insistence on mystery. What are we to make of this?

A first thing to note is that on the whole this is an image that lends itself to assertion rather than argument. How do we know that things fall into this pattern, that the many really do flow out from or point in towards a single center? For the most part, it seems, this is not a claim that Balthasar can establish step by step, but one which he simply announces.

35. *Theo-Drama*, Volume 4: *The Action*, trans. Graham Harrison (San Francisco: Ignatius, 1994), p. 240.

In some cases, indeed, the radiating circle imagery is quite explicitly linked to a rejection of any careful delineation of relationships. Consider for instance the connections among the thinkers Balthasar surveys in the second and third volumes of *The Glory of the Lord*. The twelve are very different, but this is only to be expected: "The very richness of God in Christ would lead us to expect [the beholding of the glory of the Lord] to occur in the most diverse ways."[36] Balthasar portrays them, then, as so many lines or rays coming out from a midpoint. What is interesting, however, is that he uses such language precisely at points where he is suggesting that the twelve do not fit into any kind of neat order. He writes, for instance, that "each original form breaks out anew from the centre"[37] in the context of rejecting the notion that he should narrate a single line of development of doctrine through them, or again that "In the new constellations of intellectual history there break out from time to time from the midpoint which is beyond history new and original perceptions" just after speaking of a "fundamental discontinuity" between the twelve.[38] There are connections and dialogues to be had between them — which he leaves to the reader to discover — but these cannot all be fit into any system.[39] Balthasar does not offer any kind of account of how the historical thought-forms derive from the "midpoint which is beyond history" (and it is hard to see how he could do so); rather, he makes reference to the common derivation from a transcendent center precisely to *reject* the need to give any particular account of the relationship between them. His use of this image, then, is not so much associated with an effort to set out concretely how the theologies in question are related, as it is with a denial of the need to discuss concrete relationships.

Again, consider Balthasar's deployment of the radiating circle image in the second volume of *Theo-Drama,* in a passage immediately following a reference to "the oft-quoted theological pluralism of the Bible":

> Naturally the standpoint of the word of God must be so total and so rich that it mocks every attempt to tie it down to particular schemata.

36. *Clerical Styles,* p. 13.
37. Ibid., p. 29.
38. Ibid., p. 20.
39. Ibid., p. 22.

All we can do is to circle around it, approaching it from countless perspectives. That is evidently why the Spirit inspired the variety of biblical writings. Neither in the forward march of the Old Testament nor in the great synthetic utterances of the New can these writings be "systematically" shown to coincide, if by "system" we mean some totality that can be cited, surveyed and evaluated before the judgment seat of human reason. On the other hand, their convergence is so evident that every new contribution is gratefully accepted as complementing our understanding of the totality, which is always richer than we thought.[40]

Here, once again, there is the link between Balthasar's deployment of the radiating circle image (or language very suggestive of it — the circling around from countless perspectives, the convergence of diverse writings) and the refusal of any concrete, reasoned account of how the things which differ (in this case, differing theological visions within the Bible) are related. To give such an account, it seems, would be to systemize. Instead one simply recognizes, as something "evident," that they converge.

There is of course no reason to suppose that every statement in theology ought to be supported by detailed, reasoned argument; there is no need, that is, to rule out the legitimacy of a theologian sometimes simply gesturing towards a way of thinking which, once articulated, will seem obvious. Conceiving of twelve theologians as so many rays from a single center seems relatively unproblematic, for instance, at least within an ecclesial context. It is perfectly natural for one working deliberately within the Christian tradition to presume without much argument that important theological visions must have some root in revelation, and if such visions are obviously very different one from the other, to see them as distinct rays from a single center seems entirely reasonable. It is not my intention to suggest that in every case where one finds Balthasar using the radiating circle image without detailed argument, something intellectually illegitimate must be going on. And yet the sheer frequency with which we come across this pattern of thought in Balthasar is enough to give pause. Might the invocation of a radiating circle, particu-

---

40. *Dramatis Personae: Man in God,* pp. 78-79.

larly when its center is transcendent and we must resist any urge to systematize its rays — might such a pattern of thought not become a more or less effortless method of waving away or rising above any situation of conflict or pluralism of ideas? For if the center is truly transcendent, then it must be impossible in principle to trace the relation of each ray to it; and if the rays meet *only* in the center, then their meeting itself, the fact that they do cohere with one another, is itself shrouded in mystery.

Let us set aside for the moment, however, any such worries about lack of argument. Is there perhaps a much more positive light in which we might consider the way this image works in Balthasar? One way to look at the recurring presence of these radiating circle images might be that in fact it counts against the broader criticism of Balthasar I am developing, showing it, indeed, to be at its root mistaken. Does not Balthasar's use of these images constantly indicate in fact that he has a *modest* conception of what a theologian can do, that he renounces the possibility of anything like a definitive overview or a single privileged perspective? If at key moments, whether in a discussion of revelation, or the Word of God, or Christ, or Christ's passion, we find Balthasar returning to the radiating circle, does he not thereby indicate the ungraspability of the thing under discussion, the inescapability of multiple perspectives, and therefore the necessarily limited and partial nature of any particular theology? Should not his use of this image, then, be understood as indicating a generous and open approach, one which allows for the existence of different perspectives on what is most important without thinking of them as coming into conflict or competition with each other?

In support of such a view one might point to the tremendous efforts Balthasar expended on making available to his contemporaries the thought of others. As we saw in Chapter Two, not only did he write monographs on Origen, Gregory of Nyssa, and Maximus, and dedicate two volumes of *The Glory of the Lord* to studies of twelve figures, but he also devoted tremendous time and energy to translating, editing, and publishing the writings of a wide range of thinkers. Here is the work, one might say, of someone who really does believe, not that he himself has the last word and the definitive overview, but that the one transcendent central point of theology needs expressing through a multiplicity of "rays."

The difficulty with such a reading, however, is the fact that *in* his very affirmation of the fragmentariness, the perspectival nature, of all theology, Balthasar frequently positions himself *above* it. This is in a sense implicit in the very image of the radiating circle — for only the one who stands *over* both the transcendent midpoint and all the rays which come out of or point in towards it, would seem to be in a position to identify the radiating circle *as* a radiating circle, to see both the rays, the central point and the relationship of all these to each other. On the one hand with this image, then, Balthasar seems to be telling us that there is no definitive overview, no single privileged perspective, that no theological vision can ever be more than a ray from the center, and yet on the other hand, in his very *ability* to tell us this, to present us with this multiplicity *as* a series of rays converging on a single mysterious center, he in fact presumes an overview of a whole range of perspectives and of their relationship to the core.

Consider, for instance, the twelve theologians dealt with in the second and third volumes of *The Glory of the Lord*. These, as we saw, Balthasar pictures as so many rays coming out of a center which lies outside history. How does Balthasar place *himself* in relation to these rays? On the one hand there seems to be humility: they are acknowledged as great lights, important, influential, they are in some sense theological guides, and he devotes many pages to the thought of each. But at the same time Balthasar seems to be writing from a perch above them, a perch that puts him in a position to survey them all, together with the center from which they emanate. Thus the examination of the twelve theologies, which is a study of a series of rays emanating from a midpoint, is to *be followed by* a treatment of the midpoint itself: by the end of the volumes dealing with these figures "we shall only have circled round the Biblical and dogmatic meaning of the glory of the Lord and have not elucidated it from the very centre. . . . But that [elucidation] will be the concern of the third volume."[41]

But is all this to make too much of a bit of imagery, which might be read as saying little more than that Balthasar believes in engagement

---

41. *Clerical Styles*, p. 30. What is called the third volume *(Band)* in German actually comprises the final four physical volumes, i.e., *The Glory of the Lord*, Volumes 4-7.

with both tradition and Scripture? Let us turn to another example of the radiating circle image that we have already mentioned. As we have seen, Balthasar refers to Jesus' "hour" in terms of mystery and transcendence, and writes of a multiplicity of New Testament and later theologies "circling around a transcendent core." The issue here is the meaning of the Cross, of the Passion and death of Christ. It is the standard fare of introductory lectures on the atonement to point to the pluralism of Scripture and tradition on this topic — to point to the fact that there is no one model or theory of the atonement presented in the New Testament, nor in the subsequent tradition. Balthasar is, then, placing this multiplicity in relation to, and explaining it by, the richness, the mystery, of that which is under question: it is natural, inevitable perhaps, that there should be a range of theologies which circle around the one thing, because that which they aim for is a transcendent mystery.

What is interesting is how Balthasar proceeds from this point. There are three main steps. First, in a very few pages he sets out five aspects — the "main features" — of the New Testament presentation of the atonement.[42] Then, following a brief and relatively abstract discussion of three ways soteriology can go wrong (by allowing one aspect to dominate over the others, by dissolving the tension between the differing aspects, or by replacing all this with something supposedly more intelligible to a particular epoch but which "in fact lacks the center of gravity of the biblical assertion"),[43] Balthasar offers a survey of the history of soteriology in some eighty pages. He ranges over patristic, medieval, and modern models, by and large showing some appreciation for each and the way it takes up one or more of the aspects, but in each case[44] also pointing to what is limited, or missing, or not as developed

42. *The Action,* pp. 240-43. The five aspects are, very briefly, as follows. (1) "Self-immolation" or self surrender: Jesus not only obediently allows himself to be handed over by the Father, but also actively surrenders himself, lays down his life; (2) Exchange: Jesus exchanges place with us; (3) We are liberated from something; (4) We are positively drawn into the divine life; (5) The whole process must be attributed to God's love.

43. Ibid., p. 243.

44. The only exception is in the final two authors he mentions — Bulgakov and Feuillet — who have "approached the mystery of vicarious suffering with great circumspection" (ibid., p. 313).

as it might be.[45] And then, finally, in a 106-page section entitled "Dramatic Soteriology," Balthasar presents what is essentially his own account of the atonement — an account which is "dramatic," as Balthasar presents it, in part because it holds in tension the various different biblical aspects of the atonement without synthesizing them or explaining them away.

To put it briefly, then, we find the following situation: first Balthasar insists that there is a mystery which cannot be synthesized, and which is therefore naturally encircled by a multiplicity of theologies; he then *evaluates* each of these theologies (at least the post-biblical ones), telling us what is to be learned, and what the deficiencies of each are; and finally he presents us with something which he suggests succeeds where all the others have failed. In other words, he can not only see how each of the rays points towards the core, but he can see how each does not do justice to it, and can go beyond them all. He places himself, not as one more ray coming out from the center, but as the spectator who stands above, the commentator who can explain how everything, human and divine, theology and revelation, mystery and its manifold expressions, fits together.

What comes out here, then, is that there is a sense in which Balthasar's theology is almost at war with itself. On the one hand we find the profound insistence on theological humility, and on the impossibly rich, transcendent, mysterious nature of the subject matter; but on the other hand there is Balthasar's theological procedure, which silently presumes his own comprehensive grasp and control of the material.

---

45. So for instance the Fathers did not do full justice to the first aspect (Christ's surrender), Anselm undervalued the second (the exchange), Luther was in difficulties as regards the fifth aspect (God's love), some modern thinkers again do not do justice to the first aspect. See pp. 317-18 of *The Action* for Balthasar's brief summary of the results of his historical survey.

CHAPTER 5

The Trinity

We turn now to the first of our extended case studies, a consideration of Balthasar's theology of the Trinity. One of the most distinctive aspects of Balthasar's thought lies here, especially in the integration of his reflections on the Trinity — on the eternal, inner life of the Trinity — into the fabric of his theology.

The distinctiveness of Balthasar in this regard can perhaps best be seen by way of contrast. A good deal of the theology of the last four or five decades has been preoccupied with the question of what to do with the doctrine of the Trinity: how can we make clear the relevance of a doctrine which surely ought to be central, but which, with its "substance" and "hypostasis," its "processions" and "relations," can seem like nothing but a series of technicalities and intellectual difficulties?[1] In Balthasar's case what is striking is not that he has a really good answer to this question, but that the question just does not need to be raised. One finds in his theology, that is to say, a vivid depiction of the inner life of the Trinity which is genuinely *integral* to his presentation of the story of salvation. Whether he ultimately has the right to such a vivid picture of the eternal life of God is a question I shall be asking, as is also whether the integration he achieves requires too resolved a vision — too positive a vision, indeed — of suffering and evil. To begin with, however, we need to give sim-

---

1. Cf. Karen Kilby, "Perichoresis and Projection: Problems with Social Doctrines of the Trinity," *New Blackfriars* 81 (2000): 432-45 for a discussion of this concern and the dominant response to it.

ply some indication of the way Balthasar interweaves (to use the usual terms) economic and immanent Trinity.

Mission Christology

One place this interweaving can be seen is in Balthasar's Christology, particularly in his presentation of an "outline of Christology" in the third volume of the *Theo-Drama*.[2] What Balthasar highlights as the central, defining feature of Jesus' life is his sense of mission, and this, particularly when coupled with an insistence on Jesus' absolute identification with this mission, sets the stage for a striking link between a reading of the historical life of Jesus and classic conceptions of the Son's eternal procession from the Father.

"The words of the Gospels point concentrically to his [Jesus'] peerless sense of mission."[3] That his mission is central to Jesus is something Balthasar takes to stand out particularly clearly in the Gospel of John, but also to be attested in the synoptic gospels and indeed throughout the New Testament. It is central, and it is linked with who Jesus is: "In the most diverse places and layers of the text, the concept of Jesus' mission appears linked with his highest qualification as 'Son of God,' as the latter's 'Beloved Son.'"[4] Both the language of Jesus as one who is sent (e.g., "he who receives you receives me, and he who receives me receives him who sent me" [Matt. 10:40]), and the language of Jesus as "coming" or "having come," are bound up with Jesus having a mission from the Father. The centrality of Jesus' sense of mission in his consciousness is also something, Balthasar maintains, which one must suppose in order to make sense of Jesus' apocalyptic sayings — his expectation of an imminent end of the world.

Balthasar does not, however, stop with the claim that Jesus has a very strong sense of mission, or that this sense of mission is particularly

---

2. *Theo-Drama*, Volume 3: *The Dramatis Personae: Persons in Christ*, trans. Graham Harrison (San Francisco: Ignatius, 1992), pp. 59-262.

3. Ibid., p. 26. Readers will note the characteristic imagery here.

4. Ibid., p. 150.

central to him, but wants rather to *identify* Jesus with his mission. Jesus does not just have a mission — he *is* the mission.

To fill out this last claim we need to look a little further at Balthasar's notion of "person" and how this relates to his understanding of mission. In a rather broad-ranging discussion, he distinguishes the question of *what* we are from the question of *who* we are. We all share the same "what," as human beings, but how is one to know *who* one is: how am I to know, that is to say, what it is that makes me distinct from others? This question of being a "who," of being someone distinct, Balthasar identifies with being a person.

One possibility for working out who one is might be to define oneself by one's distinguishing features: "He [the conscious subject] can amass empirical characteristics that are distinctive of him, that circle around his individuality." But this is unsatisfactory because it does not take us farther than "an accumulation of chance details." Another possibility is to rely on other people, to whom one is of value and special. Again, according to Balthasar, although somewhat better, this will still be unsatisfactory: not only can the regard of others be withdrawn, but "The most emphatic affirmation can only tell him who he is *for the one who values him* or loves him." Ultimately, the guarantee of who one is can only come from God:

> It is when God addresses a conscious subject, tells him who he is and what he means to the eternal God of truth and shows him the purpose of his existence — that is, imparts a distinctive and divinely authorized mission — that we can say of a conscious subject that he is a "person."[5]

Being a "who" (having a distinct identity), being a person, and being given a purpose, a mission, by God, are all then, on Balthasar's account, the same thing.

This connection between person and mission, which is true in general, is also true in Christ.[6] But there is a difference. In general, one is

5. Ibid., pp. 204-7, here p. 207.

6. Indeed, Balthasar would say, it is true in general only because it is true in Christ: "Others can claim to be persons only in virtue of a relationship with him and in dependence on him" (ibid.).

first a conscious subject, and then at some stage "called" to a mission, and so struggles to become, to grow into, the person one already is in God's sight; we undergo a process of "bringing our innate nonidentity into an ever-closer approximation to perfect identity,"[7] of assimilating "our own 'I' more and more completely to our God-given mission."[8] In the case of Christ, however, there is, from the beginning, an absolute identity. He is, at all times, fully identified with his sense of mission. So whereas we may have a mission, and strive to let our identities be conformed to it, Christ *is* his mission. Jesus is the one, then, "in whom Person and mission are identical."[9]

This identity of person and mission is linked, in Balthasar's presentation, with Christ's divinity: "the Subject in whom person and mission are identical," he writes (without, it must be admitted, much in the way of explanation), "can only be divine."[10] What is significant, from a Trinitarian point of view, is the fact that Balthasar does not arrive at Christ's divinity directly, but by way of this notion of mission. What distinguishes Jesus from the rest of us is not some abstract quality or perfection, but his relation to the Father; and it is not just his relation to the Father in general, conceived perhaps in terms of love or closeness or dependence, but concretely his relation to the Father as being sent, as having a mission.

In classic formulations of the doctrine of the Trinity, the Father is described as the "unoriginate origin," and the Son (as also the Spirit) as coming out from, proceeding from, him.[11] In seeing mission as central to the New Testament portrayals of Jesus, and indeed to Jesus' self-consciousness, then, Balthasar is developing his Christology from the start so that it will be integrated into an account of the immanent Trinity: the centrality for Jesus of mission, of being sent by the Father,

---

7. Ibid., p. 270.
8. Ibid., p. 271.
9. Ibid., p. 157.
10. Ibid., p. 157.
11. "Proceeding," as distinct from "begetting," is a general term which can be used both of Son and Spirit in relation to the Father. It is interesting that Balthasar is more inclined to focus on the notion of the Son "proceeding from" the Father than his "being begotten of" the Father here. It is perhaps easier to connect "mission" as Balthasar is using it in this context to procession than it would be to connect mission to begetting.

in other words, reflects, or is the incarnate working out of, the Son's eternal proceeding from the Father.[12]

By going so far as actually to identify Jesus' person with his mission, Balthasar is, furthermore, offering a still more striking integration. In an account such as one finds, for instance, in Thomas Aquinas, not only are the relations of the Persons of the Trinity described in terms of processions — the Son is generated by the Father, the Spirit spirated from Father and Son — but the Persons simply *are* these relations. This seems, normally, one of the more ungraspable aspects of Trinitarian thought, and I am not persuaded that Thomas himself tries to present it in such a way that we can in fact get a grasp on it.[13] But in his Christology Balthasar offers quite a concrete working out of this: Jesus is the person who so completely accepts, lives out, and identifies with his mission, that whereas others may have a mission, he simply *is* his mission. If one follows Balthasar to the point of saying that Jesus is the one in whom Person and mission are identical, then it will not perhaps seem such a conundrum to say that the eternal Son just *is* his processing from the Father.

Balthasar's development of a mission Christology, then, is impressive. He manages to unite what can seem one of the most odd and intractable features of Trinitarian theology with a quite textually concrete reading of the life of Jesus, and to do this in a way, incidentally, which is connected to his larger dramatic scheme (for one's mission is one's divinely given *role*) and which allows him to integrate anthropology into his Christology (for he maintains that all others find both their mission and their existence as persons through inclusion in Christ).

12. Standard Thomistic thought does, it should be said, make a connection between mission and procession: the mission, the sending of Son and Spirit into the world, is related to their eternal procession from the Father. Though what Balthasar is doing may sound familiar, however, it actually goes well beyond this standard position, since he is giving to "mission" a much fuller and more concrete meaning, one that has to do with the psychology of Jesus and which is related to broader notions of vocation.

13. Cf. my "Aquinas, the Trinity, and the Limits of Understanding," in the *International Journal of Systematic Theology* 7 (2005): 414-27 for an argument along these lines.

Trinity and Cross

We saw in the previous chapter that Balthasar highlights as "the quintessence of Scripture"[14] five biblical motifs surrounding the Cross (self-surrender, exchange, liberation, our being drawn into the divine life, God's love as the primary source of the whole). And we saw that in his survey of the tradition he presented each of his predecessors as having taken up some but not all of the motifs, or else having failed to maintain the appropriate balance between them. Balthasar in fact proposes that two things are needed in order to do justice to the full range of motifs. One, we have already seen, is a dramatic approach, which can keep in play and hold in tension a variety of elements, rather than attempting to reduce everything to any single concept. The second, which is our concern here, is what he calls a "Trinitarian substructure."[15]

What, then, is this Trinitarian substructure? It has to do with the nature of the relations between the Persons of the Trinity. These relations Balthasar characterizes not only in the familiar terms of love and gift, but also in terms of distance (in fact, infinite distance), otherness, risk, and kenosis.

Now, the language of the Father giving everything, giving indeed himself, to the Son, is very common in traditional Trinitarian reflection. What is far less familiar is the way Balthasar consistently glosses this giving as a giving *up*, giving *away*, a self-stripping: "the Father strips himself, without remainder, of his Godhead and hands it over to the Son";[16] the Father "can give his divinity away";[17] the Father "lets go of his divinity"; this is an "original self-surrender" in which the Father "must go to the very extreme of self-lessness."[18]

---

14. *Theo-Drama*, Volume 4: *The Action*, trans. Graham Harrison (San Francisco: Ignatius, 1994), p. 317. In German, the "Quintessenz der Schrift" (*Theodramatik*, Band III, *Die Handlung*, p. 295). For the five motifs, see note 42 of Chapter Four, above.

15. *The Action*, p. 332. The two proposals are not unrelated, for Balthasar suggests that only with this Trinitarian substructure can one be genuinely dramatic in the sense of avoiding "all the one-sidedness found in the historico-theological systems" (ibid.).

16. Ibid., p. 323.

17. Ibid., p. 325.

18. Ibid.

Where classic treatments of the Trinity tend, if anything, to emphasize the closeness, the inseparability, of the Persons, Balthasar writes repeatedly of distance (in his more cautious moments, of "something like distance") between them, of otherness and separation. The Son is "the infinitely Other" of the Father;[19] there is "an absolute, infinite 'distance'"[20] between them, "a unique and incomprehensible 'separation' of God from himself."[21] Interestingly, where in classic treatments, the closeness, the inseparability, of the Persons tends to be conceived as linked to the fullness of the Father's self-gift — because the Father gives everything he is to the Son, there can be no distance between them — in Balthasar's thought this same self-gift of the Father's (though here conceived as self-stripping) leads, it would seem, in precisely the opposite direction: Balthasar's assertion of the infinite difference or separation of the Persons regularly follows references to the Father giving himself away completely to the Son.

Kenosis — self-emptying — begins, then, not in the Cross or the Incarnation, but in the Father's generation of the Son.[22] The Father does not actually do away with himself in this kenosis: "the Father, in uttering and surrendering himself without reserve, does not lose himself. He does not extinguish himself by self-giving."[23] Nevertheless, Balthasar is keen to preserve something like a sense of risk, something vulnerable and dangerous, in this giving away.

What such an understanding of the inner relations of the eternal divine Persons does is to allow Balthasar to develop a Trinitarian understanding of the meaning of the Cross, which can then be seen not as a breach in or a change to the eternal inner-Trinitarian relations, but as an expression of them. He is able, that is, to present the Cross as the enact-

---

19. Ibid. ("as undendliche Andere" — *Theodramatik*, Band III, p. 302).

20. Ibid., p. 323 ("absoluten unendlichen Abstands" — *Theodramatik*, Band III, p. 301).

21. Ibid., p. 325 ("eine unfaßbare und unüberbietbare 'Trennung' Gottes von sich selbst" — *Theodramatik*, Band III, p. 302).

22. In this notion of an original kenosis of the Father, and therefore in fact in his whole approach to the "Trinitarian substructure" of the Cross, Balthasar is following Sergei Bulgakov, a controversial Russian theologian who died in 1944 and whose work he cites at the end of the historical outline.

23. *The Action*, p. 325.

ment of a drama between the Father and the Son, while at the same time insisting, with the tradition, that God is not somehow altered through an engagement with history.

The Cross should not be understood, Balthasar insists, simply as God incarnate, in his human nature, undergoing suffering and death on behalf of or in place of sinners. Such a statement may not be false, but it does not go far enough, does not get to the most profound level of what is at stake. It is not just God incarnate who undergoes the Cross, but *the Son*, and what is undergone is not just suffering and death, but more profoundly forsakenness, abandonment, rejection, *by the Father*. On the Cross we see God rejected by and alienated from God. On the Cross the relationship between God's wrath and sin is played out between the Father and the Son, and therefore taken over *into* God, into the relationship between the Father and the Son. But because of what we have seen above, of the infinite distance, the "incomprehensible separation" which all along, so to speak, characterizes the Father/Son relations, this is not the introduction of something *new* into the Trinity. The alienation between the sinner and an angry God can be taken into the Trinity because infinite distance and something like alienation were always already there. The Trinity, one could say a little crudely, is "big enough" to encompass and so overcome even the terrible distance between the righteous and angry God and the lost sinner.

Balthasar's much debated proposal concerning Holy Saturday is essentially the working out of this same idea.[24] What happens in the time between Christ's death and his resurrection, between Good Friday and Easter Sunday? There is a biblical reference (1 Peter 3:19; 4:6) to Christ's preaching to the dead, and traditionally this has been developed into a notion of a victorious descent, "the beginning of the manifestation of his triumph over death and the first application of the fruits of redemp-

---

24. Long recognized as one of the more idiosyncratic elements in Balthasar's thought, this has recently received intensified attention as a result of Alyssa Lyra Pitstick's argument, in *Light in Darkness: Hans Urs von Balthasar and the Catholic Doctrine of Christ's Descent into Hell* (Grand Rapids: Eerdmans, 2007), that it is simply heretical. To get some indication of the controversy this work has stirred up, see Pitstick's exchange with Edward Oakes in *First Things* 168 (December 2006) and the flood of correspondence it generated in subsequent issues.

tion."[25] Balthasar proposes, by contrast, that Christ is utterly passive on Holy Saturday, that he can no longer act, that he is genuinely dead in solidarity with the dead, and indeed that, having become identified with sin itself, he experiences the full horror of it, which is to say hell, utter rejection, and abandonment by the Father.

Balthasar's soteriology is powerful and vivid. It seems to show how we can take seriously the gravity of sin, and the recurrent biblical theme of divine wrath against sin, while presenting a drama in which the overwhelming theme is still that of God's love. It takes up the traditional themes (typically emphasized in Protestant theology) of Christ's substitution for us, even of Christ bearing punishment for us,[26] but because of the thoroughly Trinitarian way in which Balthasar sets out the drama, the usual difficulty of these themes — that a requirement for a perfectly just man to be killed for the iniquities of the unjust is repellent, arbitrary, unfair — is, if not entirely eliminated, at least reduced. The dominant sense one is left with is not of God insisting on punishing one party instead of another, but of God taking into his own life the necessary conflict between sin and love. And because Balthasar presents his soteriology not as the provision of an explanation, but as the exploration of a drama, he is able to put the emphasis on bringing out, rather than dissolving, conflicting themes and forces.

Our main concern at this stage, however, is not in his soteriology for its own sake, but in Balthasar's treatment of the Trinity, and particularly the way he interweaves reflections on the Trinity with soteriology. To appreciate the distinctiveness of this integration, it is useful to compare it to what has become in recent years the more typical pattern of Trinitarian reflection.

As I mentioned in the opening paragraph of the chapter, many con-

---

25. Pitstick, "Balthasar, Hell, and Heresy: An Exchange," *First Things* (December 2006), p. 168.

26. Balthasar is careful here: given that Christ is just, it would perhaps not be right to say that he is punished; however, he bears our burden, and "in no way distances himself from those who by rights should have to bear it" (*The Action*, p. 337). Balthasar reconciles these two points by distinguishing between an objective and a subjective sense of punishment: "Subjectively . . . he can experience it as 'punishment,' although objectively speaking, in his case, it cannot be such" (ibid., p. 338).

temporary theologians feel the need to restore the doctrine of the Trinity to a place of centrality and importance, to restore to it a sense of relevance, to rescue it from the realm of technical puzzles, intellectual gymnastics, celestial mathematics. One very common strategy is to reject the traditional Western "psychological analogy" for the Trinity[27] and introduce instead a social analogy: the Trinity is to be modeled, not on the multiple faculties or multiple activities of a single mind, but on a small community bound together by love. The relevance of the Trinity is then found in the way it becomes itself a model for community, and in the quality of the relationships within it, relationships so profound that they can make the Three genuinely One. If the doctrine of the Trinity portrays the divine in its innermost reality as Persons-in-relation, as relationships so profound that they constitute the Persons, or as relationships so profound that they lead to a "perichoretic"[28] unity of Persons, then surely it has something to say about how we think about family, about the Church, about society at all levels, and about ourselves. In this way the Trinity is found to be, after all, an edifying doctrine with a range of very practical applications.

Social theories are, of course, varied, but many share in a basic pattern, a pattern of abstraction followed by application. One moves away from the complexities of the biblical texts, away from discussions of creation, Incarnation, Cross, resurrection, ascension, Pentecost, to rest one's focus on a set of quite abstract concepts — concepts of Persons, relations, and perichoresis — and then, taking these to be what are at the heart of the doctrine of the Trinity, one looks to find application for the concepts, to give these abstractions relevance. So one can find a Colin

---

27. Augustine, in his *De Trinitate*, experimented with thinking about the three-in-oneness of God as in some way analogous to the multiple faculties, or activities, of a single mind, and particularly the activities of remembering, willing, and loving. The analogy was taken up (and often hardened) by subsequent theologians in the western theological tradition, and has come to be known, not very felicitously, as the "psychological analogy" or "psychological model" of the Trinity.

28. "Perichoresis" means the mutual indwelling of the persons of the Trinity. Many recent social theorists have been particularly fascinated by this concept. See my "Perichoresis and Projection" for a brief discussion and critique of the phenomenon, and Ryan Messmore's "Rethinking the Appeal to Perichoresis in Contemporary Trinitarian Political Theology" (unpublished D.Phil. thesis, Oxford, 2010) for a thorough and decisive critique.

Gunton, for instance, writing enthusiastically about the applications of the notion of perichoresis in metaphysics or in conceiving of the interpenetration of different academic disciplines, or a Jürgen Moltmann drawing on the eternal relations of the Trinity as a way to provide a model for Church polity and indeed a way to move beyond the impasse between Western individualism and Eastern communitarianism.

On some points Balthasar is at one with these social theorists. He too envisages the Persons of the Trinity functioning as something not too far from persons in our ordinary sense of the term,[29] and so he too imagines the Trinity as something closer to a small society or family than to differing aspects of a single psyche. But here the ways part, for Balthasar does not engage in the abstraction so characteristic of social theories of the Trinity. The Trinity is never, in Balthasar's theology, a doctrine in search of a meaning, and he does not need to propose for it some extra relevance of its own: it is rather, as he presents it, intimately concerned with, and necessary for the understanding of, the life of Jesus and particularly the Cross. So, for example, though Balthasar is like the social theorists in showing a concern with the eternal inner relations of the Trinity, he leads us not into a reflection about a general concept of relations that can then perhaps find useful application elsewhere, but into a reflection very specifically about the relation of the Father to the Son (and to some extent of the Holy Spirit to both).[30] We have in Balthasar, then, as vivid and gripping a presentation of the inner life of the Trinity as any social theorist could wish for, but one which maintains at every stage vital links with the drama of salvation.

29. Cf. "Perichoresis and Projection" for the case that this is one of the key distinguishing marks of social Trinitarians.

30. Balthasar in my judgment shares in the weakness of much modern western theology when it comes to the role of the Spirit. Something is always said about the Third Person of the Trinity, some role envisaged, but it can easily appear as a kind of afterthought, an addendum; the Spirit rarely seems as central and necessary to the account as are Father and Son.

Too Vivid?

Balthasar portrays the immanent Trinity, then, in a way which is vivid and powerful. There is eternal kenosis, infinite difference, distance, and otherness which is nevertheless united in love, a "primal drama." But does he have a right to be so vivid? We turn now to the question of how Balthasar can know what he appears to know about the Trinity, and indeed what exactly some of his language about the Trinity might mean.[31]

Insofar as Balthasar provides an explicit account of a method of Trinitarian reflection, there seems little to which one might object. Like most theologians, Balthasar maintains that we learn of the Trinity not through philosophical reflection on God and the world, but through Christ:

> It is only on the basis of Jesus Christ's own behavior and attitude that we can distinguish such a plurality in God. Only in him is the Trinity opened up and made accessible.[32]

31. One question that I will not attempt to deal with here is whether Balthasar is in fact propounding tritheism. This is a concern to which his theology, like that of the social theorists discussed above, can give rise. In both cases the Persons of the Trinity seem to be presented as three centers of consciousness, three "I's" with three wills which are, in principle at least, distinct. One can find in Balthasar's writings texts which seem to suggest that the Persons of the Trinity in some sense "arrive" at an agreement about what to do: thus, for instance, "Since each Person of the Trinity enjoys the one divine will in divine freedom, a decision in God can only come about through the *mutual integration* of the Persons' 'points of view'" (*Theo-Drama*, Volume 5: *The Last Act*, trans. Graham Harrison [San Francisco: Ignatius, 1998], p. 95).

The reason I will not take up this issue here is that it seems to me that Trinitarian theology of the last century and this one has arrived at a kind of stand-off in this area. One finds a sharp divide between those, like Barth and Rahner, who think that the term "Person" has become misleading in a Trinitarian context, and reach for some other technical term to discuss what is threefold in God (e.g., manner of subsisting or mode of being) and those who take there to be real continuity between our contemporary understanding of "person" and the Trinitarian Persons. And on each side of this divide there is suspicion of the orthodoxy of the other. If there is a question about whether the social theorists and Balthasar are advocating tritheism, there can also be a question as to whether the other side is in fact modalist, denying the reality of the Three in God. The debate is a little too big for me to enter into here in a helpful way.

32. *Persons in Christ*, p. 508.

This insistence on the centrality of Jesus to our understanding of the Trinity is affirmed at a number of points:

> The revelation of the Trinity is bound to Jesus Christ, to his self-giving and hence to his consciousness.[33]

> We must hold fast to the conviction that the Trinity is not a synthesis of monotheism (Judaism) and polytheism (Hellenism) but only comes to light with the figure of Jesus Christ.[34]

As will be clear from what has already been outlined, more than many theologians, Balthasar lays particular emphasis on the *Cross* as revelatory of the Trinity. But there seems little reason, a priori, to object to this, given the centrality of the Cross in the gospel accounts and indeed in Christian belief and practice. And, finally, we should note that at certain points Balthasar makes explicit gestures in the direction of epistemological humility: he writes, for instance:

> On the basis of what is manifest in God's kenosis in the theology of the covenant — and thence in the theology of the Cross — we *must feel our way back into the mystery* of the absolute, employing a negative theology that excludes from God all intramundane experience and suffering, while at the same time presupposing that the possibility of such experience and suffering . . . is grounded in God. *To think in such a way is to walk on a knife edge.*[35]

One can find, on this level, an acknowledgment of the difficulty and the precariousness of reflection on the immanent Trinity.

The problem here does not become clear, then, from what Balthasar *says* about how one should reflect on the Trinity. To see the problem one needs to look once again at how he in fact proceeds. Let us consider, for instance, Balthasar's language of distance in the Trinity. Between the Fa-

---

33. Ibid., p. 509.
34. Ibid., p. 512.
35. *The Action,* p. 324, emphasis added.

ther and the Son, united though they are in love, Balthasar maintains, there is an infinite distance. This is, as we have already suggested, a relatively novel claim. It is not, or at least it has not traditionally been thought to be, something that self-evidently follows from standard affirmations about ousia and hypostases, processions and relations.

How, then, does Balthasar think we know of this infinite distance, separation, otherness, in the Trinity? There are two routes by which he arrives at this point. One — perhaps the less important one — has to do with the avoidance of modalism. Balthasar seems to suggest that something like distance, or "infinite space"[36] must be necessary for the distinction between the Trinitarian Persons to be real. The second route, more frequently stressed, is by way of the Cross: we do not, he thinks, know of this inner-Trinitarian distance *only* from the Cross, but we somehow know it better, know of its full seriousness, from the Cross: "It is only from the Cross and in the context of the Son's forsakenness that the latter's distance from the Father is fully revealed."[37]

But simply to say that we learn of this distance from the Cross is in fact a little too easy. It is not the case that one has only to look at the Passion narratives to come to the conclusion that there must, in eternity, be an infinite distance between Father and Son. Certainly this is not something that most of the tradition has in fact learned from these narratives, nor is it, I suspect, something most Christians today learn from reading them. At least two things are required in order to learn of distance in the Trinity from the Cross. The first is a particular construal of the Cross itself; the second is a more speculative move from the Cross (thus construed) to what one could call the eternal conditions of its possibility.

The first thing, then, is that one must construe the Cross, Christ's Passion and death, as most fundamentally a drama of abandonment of Christ by the Father. Although Balthasar is not alone in interpreting it in this way (for all the differences at other points, here he is fundamentally in accord with Jurgen Moltmann), this cannot pose as an obvious or unquestionable reading of the New Testament. There is, first of all, considerable scholarly

36. *Theo-Drama*, Volume 2: *Dramatis Personae: Man in God*, trans. Graham Harrison (San Francisco: Ignatius, 1990), p. 257.
37. *The Action*, p. 320.

debate over how to interpret Jesus' cry, "My God, my God, why have you forsaken me?," as recorded in Mark and Matthew: is this an expression of a sense of abandonment, or is it, as a quotation of the first line of Psalm 22, an affirmation of faith?[38] And even if one accepts the former interpretation, and remains untroubled by the fact that there seems to be no overtones of such an experience of abandonment in the accounts of Luke or John, one needs still to make a further step; one needs to move, that is, from observing that Jesus is portrayed as suffering a sense of abandonment to affirming that what is most fundamentally being depicted and played out *is* in fact the abandonment of Jesus by the Father. The abandonment, in other words, needs to be thought of, not just as an element in the experience that Jesus as a suffering and dying human being has, but rather as the underlying truth, the *central* underlying truth, of what is taking place on the Cross.

Having determined to read the Cross as a drama of God's abandonment by God, the Father's rejection of the Son, the second thing one must do to arrive at the notion of distance in the Trinity is to suppose that this abandonment on the Cross (and during Holy Saturday) is possible *only if* the eternal Trinitarian relations are characterized by infinite, absolute distance, radical otherness, separation. This is not a matter of reasoning from an effect back to its cause, exactly, but rather from a historical (or quasi-historical)[39] drama of the economic Trinity to the characteristics of its eternal ground. What must have always been the case in the relations between Father and Son if they can on the Cross be expressed in terms of abandonment of the latter by the former? To be able to answer this question, it is worth noting, one has to suppose one knows how to do a certain kind of sifting, considering the various elements of the drama of the Cross and distinguishing between those which are specifically intramundane on the one hand and those which reveal

---

38. Psalm 22 concludes with a strong avowal of faith: "To him, indeed, shall all who sleep in the earth bow down; before him shall bow all who go down to the dust, and I shall live for him. Posterity will serve him; future generations will be told about the Lord, and proclaim his deliverance to a people yet unborn, saying that he has done it." It was common practice to say the first line of a psalm in order to refer to the psalm as a whole.

39. Balthasar characterizes Christ's experience of hell on Holy Saturday as "timeless," which raises some questions about whether one can describe the event of the Cross as historical.

something of the eternal life of the Trinity on the other. One does not, for instance, directly impute rejection and forsakenness to the immanent Trinity, but one does learn of distance and separation.

What I have so far suggested, then, is that to make the move Balthasar does from the Cross to an infinite distance in the eternal life of God requires both that one adopt a particular, contested reading of the significance of the death of Jesus, and that one then make a particular deduction, from the drama of the Cross thus construed, to the eternal conditions of its possibility. None of this need be illegitimate. But what I think does emerge is that this notion of infinite, absolute distance in the Trinity cannot be put forward as a kind of obvious and self-evident starting point for further argument or reflection, but is at most the highly tentative and rather precarious conclusion to a train of theological argumentation. If we construe the Cross in a particular way, then perhaps we can indeed tentatively hypothesize something like infinite distance in the Trinity to make sense of it. But to treat this notion of inner-Trinitarian distance as though it were itself simply a given, a dogmatic datum, something to be understood with confidence, built upon, and further refined, would be illegitimate.

Another way to come to see the precarious nature of this notion is to turn to the slightly different question of what exactly it might *mean* to talk of infinite distance in the eternal Trinity.[40] It is certainly a suggestive, an evocative notion, but not on the face of it a particularly clear one. Balthasar does not, of course, propose that the Trinitarian Persons have bodies which could be located at particular points in space, and between which one could therefore measure physical distance. But if not as physical or spatial, how then are we in fact to think of this distance? Rowan Williams suggests that we might take the German here *(Abstand)* as "difference,"[41] so would we perhaps make more headway if we ask what

---

40. Of course, Balthasar, like any mainstream Catholic theologian, holds that all our language of God is analogical, and so in a sense it is *always* beyond us to say *exactly* what any word means when applied to God. But this quite general conviction of the analogical nature of all language about God should not be used to cut off any questions whatsoever about the meaning of a particular theological claim, particularly such a *novel* claim about the eternal Trinitarian relations as this one.

41. Rowan Williams, "Balthasar on the Trinity," *The Cambridge Companion to Hans*

might be meant by the infinite, absolute *difference* between Father and Son? This too is, prima facie, difficult to grasp, given that the Persons of the Trinity are consubstantial. That everything the Father is, he gives to the Son, is a traditional claim, and one also reaffirmed by Balthasar. The difference cannot lie in the "what" that is given, then; the only place left to locate the difference would seem to be in the fact that in one instance something is given, in the other received. The Father is the one who gives everything to the Son, the Son the one who receives everything from the Father. Can this difference, distance, separateness, of which Balthasar speaks — this *infinite* and absolute difference, distance, separateness — be a matter of the difference between total gift and total reception? Perhaps. But there is still quite a bit of room for questions.

Reflection on instances of giving that are rather more familiar might prompt one kind of hesitation. In general, we do not think of giving, and in particular giving of oneself, as creating distance, difference, separation between giver and receiver — at least not unless the giving somehow goes wrong. One might argue that it is otherwise in sexual relations, where difference and intimate giving seem in some sense to go together. We will return to this area, one very important to Balthasar, in the next chapter, but for the moment it is worth noting that even if difference is important here, sexual difference is not so much *constituted by* acts of giving and receiving, as it is (perhaps) the precondition of this particular kind of giving and receiving.

Even if we set aside such analogies as irrelevant — perhaps giving and receiving just are radically different in the sphere of the divine, or perhaps in light of the Cross and the Trinity we must reconceive all giving in terms of the creation of distance and otherness (indeed, as we shall discuss below, this is not too far from what Balthasar does propose) — even if we set all this aside, there are other difficulties lurking. The Father, according to Balthasar, empties himself, strips himself, in the originally kenotic act of giving himself to the Son, and we are exploring the possibility that it is in the difference between such kenosis and the Son's reception that the infinite distance or difference is to be found. But then

---

Urs von Balthasar, ed. Edward T. Oakes, S.J., and David Moss (Cambridge: Cambridge University Press, 2004), p. 41.

the Son is of course also engaged in kenosis — the Son follows the Father in this self-giving, self-stripping; the Son too, as image of the Father, completely gives himself away. So how can this, the difference between giving and receiving, actually constitute the otherness, the distance, the difference, between Father and Son, if self-giving is one of the things in which the Son precisely images the Father?

Again, here too perhaps answers can be found. Perhaps it is not in giving and receiving as such that one is to find the locus for the infinite, absolute difference, but the very particular relation between Father and Son that involves the one always giving and the other always receiving. Perhaps it is then *this particular* act of giving and receiving that somehow sets the two in a relation of infinite difference. The "somehow," though, needs to be distinctly stressed here.

I do not mean to suggest that we should say that language of distance or difference or separation in the eternal life of the Trinity is senseless, that it can in principle have no meaning. But certainly it seems that we find ourselves in rather difficult waters if we try to imagine what is in fact envisaged here; it is not particularly easy to offer a positive account of what "distance" or "difference," much less infinite, absolute distance or difference, might look like in the Trinity. Ultimately, it seems that the position is something like this: if the Cross is conceived as God abandoning God, and if we are not, like Moltmann, to think of it as introducing something *new*, something previously unexperienced, into the life of the Trinity, then we are bound to suppose that there is *something* eternally present in the life of the Trinity which anticipates it, something to which it gives expression. Balthasar calls this whatever-it-is that anticipates the Cross distance, but, as the explorations above suggest, that really gets us no further towards imagining what it might be than would the phrase "that inexplicable, incomprehensible X in the eternal life of the Trinity, whatever it may be, which is a condition of the possibility of the Cross."

What is striking in Balthasar's Trinitarian discussions, however, is that in a great many cases they are *not* marked by the tentativeness, the sense of precariousness, that ought to follow both from the way such notions as absolute distance are derived, and from the questions surrounding what they might mean. Instead we find confidence, ease, expansiveness, fluency — a sense that Balthasar knows very well what he is describing and is quite happy to fill out the picture. We find in him, not someone driven to stutter uncertainly, somehow, in light of the Cross, about the Trinity, but rather a theologian who seems very well to know his way around, to have a view — even sometimes something that seems remarkably like an insider's view — of what happens in the inner life of the Trinity.

Balthasar is expansive on a number of fronts. He comments relatively freely, first of all, about the mechanics of the Trinitarian processions. He affirms, for instance, not only that the Father begets the Son, but that the Son "antecedently consents" to being begotten, that he holds himself in readiness to be begotten, that Son and Spirit place themselves at the disposal of their generation.[42] He also seems to know a good deal about the attitudes of the Trinitarian Persons towards each other. Thus, he affirms that the Father is grateful to the Son for allowing himself to be begotten, who in turn is grateful to the Father for *wanting* to beget him;[43] he also tells us that surprise, "eternal amazement," is an element of the life of the Trinity, so that for instance "It is as if the Son ... 'from the outset surpasses the Father's wildest expectations,'"[44] while the Son himself is always beholding the Father from new angles. The eternal life of the Trinity is, he seems to know, characterized by thanksgiving (each hypostasis "can only be itself insofar as it endlessly affirms and gives thanks for its own existence and all that shares existence"[45]), by worship, and even by petitionary prayer.

The sense that Balthasar knows his way around the inner workings of the Trinity surprisingly well is at its strongest if one looks at the way he describes what one might call the Trinity's decision-making processes. Consider the following passage:

> If the Father has a (primary) intention — perhaps with regard to the shape of the creation he has planned — he communicates this intention to the Son in begetting him, giving him "preludes, beginnings

42. *The Last Act,* p. 86.
43. Ibid., p. 87.
44. Ibid., p. 79, quoting from von Speyr.
45. Ibid., p. 75.

taken up by the Son to be realized"; thus he leaves it to the Son to "promote the fatherly purposes." In begetting the Son, the Father, as it were, addresses a request to him, and the Son in turn wishes nothing other than to employ his entire filial freedom in fulfilling the Father's will. So "the Father is the first to ask: and he asks the Son, in order to give him the joy of granting his request. . . . Even before the Son asks him" (for instance, to be entrusted with the task of saving the world through the Cross), "the Father wants to make his request, as if to give the Son precedence in the delight of granting."[46]

The Father, then, has the broad ideas, but he leaves it to the Son (out of "consideration,"[47] a desire to give the Son a certain precedence) to work out the details of implementation. Just how concretely and seriously this division of labor is meant becomes clear in a further citation from von Speyr that Balthasar provides in a footnote: "Perhaps the Father would have had other suggestions, other ideas pertaining to redemption that would not have made the abandonment of the Cross necessary. But he does not express them; he leaves redemption up to the Son. In love, what is best is always what the other wishes."[48]

Much of what I have cited in the last two paragraphs comes from the fifth and final volume of the *Theo-Drama*, but though it is here that Balthasar waxes most eloquent (whether in his own words, or through his endorsement of those of von Speyr) about the inner life of the Trinity, it would be wrong to suppose that this late volume is somehow an aberration. We have seen some examples of quite free and confident language of divine self-stripping and a primal kenosis in the fourth volume, and one can find already in the second volume references to mutual ac-

46. Ibid., pp. 88-89, quoting from von Speyr.

47. "Thus we come to see that it 'belongs to his nature to know *consideration*. God is considerate of God'" (ibid., p. 89). Once again Balthasar is quoting from von Speyr.

48. Ibid., p. 89. Balthasar also (approvingly) quotes von Speyr to the effect that "In God everything is full of these loving details which contribute essentially to understanding the Trinity" (*The World of Prayer* [San Francisco: Ignatius, 1985], p. 65, quoted in *The Last Act*, p. 87, my emphasis). The fact that von Speyr, and following her Balthasar, seems to be in a position to know such details, and also hold that knowledge of these details is "essential," is rather extraordinary.

knowledgment, adoration, and petition among the Persons of the Trinity, the need for each to have "space," and an insistence on the "joys of expectation, hope, and fulfillment."[49] Balthasar's thinking about the Trinity and the Cross is actually remarkably consistent from the time he published *Heart of the World* in 1945 through to the end of his life.[50]

At times, as we have seen, Balthasar makes gestures of epistemic humility. At times he points to a scriptural basis, or a process of reasoning, by which he arrives at his claims about the inner life of God. But taken as a whole, he does not write like a theologian who is "feeling his way back" into a mystery, on the basis of Christ and the Cross; he writes more like a novelist[51] who, with a particular understanding of the Cross as a starting point, freely fills out background, adds character details, constructs prior scenes ("a primal drama"), and evokes a general atmosphere, all to make the central point plausible, powerful, effective — to make it work.[52]

The result is a theology that is undoubtedly integrated and vivid: integrated, because while it may not be especially plausible to claim that all Balthasar tells us of the Trinity is *derived* from Christ and the Cross, it is for the most part in one way or another *related* to Christ and the Cross, and vivid, because the larger story in which Balthasar places the Cross does serve to lend a kind of intensity to its drama. But it is also a work which seems to transgress the usual bounds of theology, to speak with too much confidence, to know more than can be known.[53]

49. *Dramatis Personae: Man in God,* pp. 257-58.

50. The striking way in which the early *Heart of the World* foreshadows Balthasar's later work is examined by Andrew Louth in "The Place of *Heart of the World* in the Theology of Hans Urs von Balthasar," in *The Analogy of Beauty: The Theology of Hans Urs von Balthasar,* ed. John Riches (Edinburgh: T&T Clark, 1986).

51. It is not out of carelessness that I am casting Balthasar here as a novelist rather than a playwright, in spite of his interest in drama and relative *dis*interest in the genre of the novel. At times he informs us *directly* about the dispositions and intentions of his (divine) characters — almost, one could say, about what it "feels like" to be the Father or Christ on the cross — and this is something that a novelist can do, but a playwright cannot.

52. Rowan Williams makes a related point, though in typically understated form: "there is an inevitable risk," he writes in an essay on Balthasar and the Trinity, "of creating a divine narrative, a story like the stories of contingent agents, of the kind that mainstream Trinitarian theology has consistently sought to avoid" ("Balthasar on the Trinity," p. 47).

53. Could one defend a genre of theology that is novelistic in the sense that I have just

Too Integrated?

The previous section focused on *how* Balthasar knows all that he seems to know, how indeed any theologian could possibly be in a position to make the claims that Balthasar does. We turn now to a more critical consideration of *what* he says. In other words, even if one might accept in principle that any such detailed and intimate portrait of the inner life of the Trinity could be acceptable, there is an aspect of Balthasar's account which ought still, I will suggest, to give significant pause. I will argue that we find in what Balthasar says of the Trinity the apex of a tendency which is in fact met at all levels in his writings, and that whatever one makes of this tendency at other points, here it is distinctly troubling.

What is this tendency? Suffering, loss, and self-abasement get a strong press in Balthasar's works. A proclivity to cast suffering in a positive light, and to link faith, love, and obedience with self-loss, self-abasement, even something like annihilation of the self, is something that constantly makes itself felt.

One can see this first of all in Balthasar's treatment of the Cross, and its extension into Holy Saturday. There is here a dwelling upon suffering, a concern to bring out the depth, the immensity, the all-exceeding quality, of Christ's agony. The interest is not primarily with Christ's physical suffering, nor with his suffering of injustice, humiliation, and betrayal on the part of authorities, disciples, and so on. Balthasar's concern pivots rather on Jesus' suffering of God's wrath, his suffering the betrayal and abandonment by the Father, the hell of absolute God-forsakenness. And he is very concerned to insist on the intensity, the unbearable, unspeakable, unthinkable *enormity*, of this suffering. Because of Christ's "filial in-

---

described? Quite possibly. Such an intellectual genre might be very useful in broadening and opening our imagination, in shaking us out of unhelpful presuppositions. So, to take one example, Balthasar tells us that there is surprise in the eternal relations of the Trinitarian Persons. How could he possibly know? And yet this is a suggestion that might serve to free us from mistaking traditional notions of divine eternity, immutability, and *apatheia* to mean that God is somehow static, immobile, dull. The very idea of an eternal surprise, in other words, may usefully unsettle us. What is problematic, however, is to engage in such novelistic theologizing without *acknowledging* that this is what one is doing. William Young's *The Shack* (Newbury Park, CA: Windblown Media, 2007) might be taken as a model of novelistic theologizing which presents itself as such.

timacy with the Father," Balthasar writes, he can "suffer *total abandonment* by the Father and taste that suffering *to the last drop*."[54] Christ's sufferings are, he tells us, "far above all sufferings entailed by sin."[55] Balthasar affirms at a number of points that the experience of Holy Saturday is timeless; Pascal is right to say that "Jesus' agony lasts until the end of the world" as is Be'rulle to speak of the eternal openness of Christ's mortal wounds.[56] Balthasar represents Christ's sufferings as exceeding and so in some sense containing all other suffering; he endorses Barth's claim that "All that happened to Israel then [in the Old Testament] and since in terms of divine judgment is 'only a faint reflection compared with the infinitely more terrible happenings that took place on Good Friday,'"[57] and writes elsewhere of "wounds which transcend all inner worldly hurts."[58] Christ's suffering "towers far above chronological time," he writes in his collection of aphorisms, and "Never will an individual man or the totality of all humanity even approximately grasp and encompass these sufferings."[59]

If the salvific suffering of Christ, and an insistence on its eternity and enormity, is important in Balthasar's theology, then so is the fact that this is something which Christ can graciously "share" with his followers. Balthasar affirms at a number of points the existence of a mystical participation in Christ's Passion, in Holy Saturday, in Christ's experience of abandonment and God-forsakenness. He is interested in the mystics' "dark night of the soul" in general, and in the experiences of Adrienne von Speyr in particular.[60]

---

54. *Truth Is Symphonic: Aspects of Christian Pluralism*, trans. Graham Harrison (San Francisco: Ignatius, 1987), p. 169, emphasis added.

55. *The Action*, p. 338.

56. Ibid., p. 337.

57. Ibid., p. 346.

58. *Elucidations*, trans. John Riches (San Francisco: Ignatius, 1998), p. 84.

59. *The Grain of Wheat: Aphorisms*, trans. Erasmo Leiva-Merikakis (San Francisco: Ignatius, 1995), p. 70.

60. It is presumably in the context of his interest in the experience of mystics that we should understand comments like the following:

> The more we come to know God, the more the difference between joy and suffering becomes tenuous: not only do both things become engulfed in the One

The importance in Balthasar's theology of Christ allowing others a share in his suffering leads at some points to distinctive and rather surprising exegetical moves. Why does Jesus weep at the death of Lazarus? This is a traditional conundrum, since, if one supposes that Jesus knows that he will raise Lazarus, there seems little cause for tears at his death. One solution that has been given in the tradition is that Jesus weeps for the suffering of Martha and Mary, and on this Balthasar puts an unusual spin of his own:

> He must have been deeply moved at the inner tragic dimension in which he had to share his God-forsakenness on the Cross (eucharistically and by way of anticipation) with those he loved in a special way.[61]

In the delay of his arrival, in other words, through his temporary "abandonment" of them, Jesus has allowed Martha and Mary to share in his own experience of divine forsakenness, and it is for this, according to Balthasar, that he weeps. Or, perhaps even more startlingly, Balthasar suggests that in the words to Mary from the cross, "Woman, this is your son," Jesus is not so much providing for his mother as *rejecting* her and so allowing her a share in his forsakenness.

If, for some, an aspect of the Christian life may be the "gift" of a share in unimaginable suffering, in Christ's Passion and God-forsakenness, the Christian life for all is fundamentally to be characterized as *surrender*. Self-abnegation, loss of self, and sacrifice of the self, are constantly to the fore in Balthasar's presentation of faith and the Christian life — and these not just as the vocation of some, or as things that faith might sometimes require, or as things that the Christian must when necessary embrace willingly, but as essential, constitutive, defining components of Christian faith and life.

Will of the Father, but love itself becomes painful, and this pain becomes an irreplaceable bliss (*Grain of Wheat*, p. 13).

This aphorism is immediately followed by the suggestion that purgatory is "perhaps the deepest but also the most blissful kind of suffering" (ibid.).

61. *Truth Is Symphonic*, pp. 131-32.

It is instructive here to consider Balthasar's treatment of Mary's fiat, her consent to the angel's message in the annunciation. This Balthasar takes to be the perfect and archetypal response of faith. "Let it be done to me according to thy will": allowing oneself to be molded and stamped by God, allowing oneself to become as wax is, for Balthasar, the perfection of faith. He is keen to insist that this is not passivity, but what he calls "active receptivity." Nevertheless, it is construed very much in terms of self-abnegation. Mary's achievement, the "highest . . . made possible by grace," is "unconditional self-surrender," "pure transparency. Pure flight from self. Pure *emptied space* for the Incarnation of the Word."[62]

The sense that suffering, self-abnegation, and indeed humiliation carry some sort of positive valuation for Balthasar is confirmed at almost every turn in his writings. If we limit ourselves to a single, relatively slender volume of essays in ecclesiology (the second volume of *Explorations in Theology*), we find references to the Church as "borne by the suffering members" to the "inner mystery of suffering" that the Constantinian church of glory hid; to the true Christian spirit as "the will to poverty, abasement and humility"; to the "real, fruitful humiliation" of Peter, which was not a "mere exercise in humiliation"; to a humility which, because we are sinners, must be "instilled into us by humiliation"; to "self-abnegation in the service of Christ" as the only way to reveal Christ's own self-abnegation; to a self-abnegation that liturgical piety requires — one which indeed Balthasar describes as "this violent, this often 'crucifying' sacrifice of the pious subject to the ecclesial object"; and to "complete self-abnegation and obedience to the hierarchy" as something Charles de Foucauld rightly commended.[63]

Even when Balthasar expresses thanks to his family, this same alignment of love and suffering makes itself felt. In a retrospective essay written in 1965, after a paragraph on the impossibility of properly acknowledging all that one ought to be thankful for, we find the following:

62. *First Glance at Adrienne von Speyr*, trans. Antje Lawry and Sergia Englund, O.C.D. (San Francisco: Ignatius, 1981), pp. 51, 52. Though the immediate context is a description of von Speyr's views, Balthasar makes it clear that they are also his own.

63. *Explorations in Theology*, Volume 2: *Spouse of the Word*, trans. A. V. Littledale, with Alexander Dru (San Francisco: Ignatius, 1991), pp. 179, 16, 14, 114, 188, 27, 30, 25.

And where would a man end, if he wanted to begin thanking those of his fellow men who accompanied him on his way, formed him, protected him, made everything possible? Left and right the greetings would have to go: to the nameable and the nameless. A mother is there, who during the course of a long fatal illness dragged herself to Church each morning to pray for her children. Other close relatives, of whom (to what ends God knows) fearful sufferings were demanded. Only in the light of God will one really know what he has to be thankful for.[64]

He is of course thanking his family for nurturing, loving, and educating him — this is presumably all covered in the first sentence cited. But what particularly calls out for gratitude here is, first, the painful prayers of one suffering and dying, and then simply sufferings whose purpose is unknown.

What are we to make of all this? Opinion will perhaps divide. Balthasar is not alone in this sensibility which aligns on some very fundamental level love and sanctity with suffering, and faith with self-abnegation. Something similar can be found in late medieval thought and practice, and in strands of Counter-Reformation and nineteenth-century piety. On the other hand, to develop such alignments is by no means an instinct which has characterized the *whole* of the Christian tradition: it is largely absent from the Fathers and from Thomas, for instance. It is a sensibility which some will take to be an authentic, developed expression of a theology of the Cross, an element of the mystical tradition that Balthasar laudably retrieves and revitalizes in the face of the shallow optimism and activism of his time and our own; and which others will find alien, and see perhaps as a masochistic distortion of Christianity.

Whatever one makes of this alignment as it pertains to the characterization of Christian faith and the Christian life, however, there is a fundamental problem when a similar alignment is imported into speculation about the inner life of the eternal Trinity — and this is in fact what we find in Balthasar.

---

64. "In Retrospect: 1965," from *My Work: In Retrospect* (San Francisco: Ignatius, 1993), p. 88.

I write of a "similar alignment" rather than "the same alignment" because Balthasar does not — quite — bring suffering into the Trinity.[65] But he does speak of something in the Trinity which can develop into suffering, of a "suprasuffering" in God, and, as we have seen, of risk, of distance, and of something "dark" in the eternal Trinitarian drama. We have seen that he consistently construes the *giving* internal to the Trinity in terms of giving *away*, giving up — in terms suggestive of loss. And we have seen that he has a kenotic understanding of the giving which makes up the Trinitarian life, so that he can speak of the Father letting go of his divinity, giving it away, surrendering himself, going "to the very extreme of self-lessness."

By bringing together in his depiction of God self-loss, self-abnegation, something that comes very close to self-annihilation on the one hand, and love on the other — or again, by bringing bliss together with something that can be described either as supra-suffering, or as that which can develop into suffering — Balthasar is fundamentally blurring the distinction between love and loss, joy and suffering. If love and renunciation, suffering (or something like it) and joy, are linked, not just in the Christian life, but eternally in God, then ultimately suffering and loss are given a positive valuation: they are eternalized, and take on an ultimate ontological status. And then, it seems to me, it becomes hard to understand how Christianity can possibly be "good news."[66]

Donald MacKinnon, an early and highly influential Anglican admirer of Balthasar, reads Balthasar as a theologian who, more than many others, reckons with the Holocaust. In an essay dealing with the Christology of the *Theo-Drama,* MacKinnon writes:

---

65. See Gerard O'Hanlon, *The Immutability of God in the Theology of Hans Urs von Balthasar* (Cambridge: Cambridge University Press, 1990), for a careful discussion of this issue.

66. I would, in other words, be inclined to judge exactly the reverse of Balthasar about the relation between darkness and God. He writes that "we have no right to regard the Trinity one-sidedly as the 'play' of an absolute 'blessedness' that abstracts from concrete pain and lacks the 'seriousness' of separation and death" (*The Action*, p. 325). I would suggest to the contrary that Christians have no right to overcome their incomprehension of evil by introducing pain, separation, and death (or something like them) into their talk of God, no right to the intellectual resolution that comes from knowing of some happening in God that "justifies the possibility and actual occurrence of all suffering in the world" (ibid., p. 324).

In the pages of his work with which we are here concerned there is comparatively little that treats directly of these horrors; but the nervous tension of the whole argument bears witness to the author's passionate concern to present the engagement of God with his world in a way that refuses to turn aside from the overwhelming, pervasive reality of evil. . . . [Balthasar] insists on a vision that can only be won through the most strenuous acknowledgment of the cost of human redemption.[67]

MacKinnon is certainly right about Balthasar's insistence on a "strenuous acknowledgment of the cost of human redemption": as we have seen, Balthasar insists on stressing the enormity, the infinite weight of what took place on Good Friday and Holy Saturday — where Christ in some sense plunges into the experience of all that is most wrong with the world and bears it himself. But we have also seen that Balthasar is concerned to root the Cross firmly in the immanent Trinity, so that there is no question of God at this particular stage taking on something new, something previously unknown (this is what Balthasar believes must be rejected of Moltmann): instead there is the working out on the Cross of something always true of the immanent Trinity. The blurring that I have described in Balthasar's thought, between bliss and suffering, between love and loss, necessarily follows from these two moves: if Christ is to take into himself all that is most wrong, and if this is not to be something new, but something always in some way anticipated in the Trinity, then it seems that there is no way to avoid importing into God's eternity something of all that is most wrong, and so introducing a sort of fusion of the highest love and the greatest bliss with (something like) the greatest suffering and the profoundest loss. In Balthasar's hands the effort to grapple in full theological seriousness with tragedy seems in great danger of finally flipping over into something like a divinizing of the tragic.[68]

---

67. "Some Reflections on Hans Urs von Balthasar's Christology with Special Reference to Theodramatik II/2 and III," in *Analogy of Beauty*, p. 165.

68. Alyssa Lyra Pitstick's *Light in Darkness* picks up well on these or closely related dangers in Balthasar's thought. In contrast to the tradition, she writes, "Balthasar seems to ascribe a positive value to suffering and death in themselves in virtue of their likeness to the suffering Redeemer, not to mention the Trinity" (p. 133). She argues very effectively,

This section is entitled "Too integrated?" and we are now in a position to see why. On the face of it, Balthasar is impressive, perhaps unsurpassed, in the integration he achieves between soteriology and Trinitarian theology. But the cost turns out to be high. The way in which Balthasar brings together reflection on the immanent Trinity and reflection on the world's horrors involves, in the end, an introduction of elements from the latter into the former, elements of darkness into the divine light. The highest love of God and the greatest misery of the world are reconciled in his thought by introducing elements of misery, destruction, and loss into the conception of love itself.

---

too, that although Balthasar may maintain that sin has no place in the Trinity, "this position remains on the level of assertion" (p. 238), in that the whole weight of his thought, both in making sin a reality in itself, and in relating it to the distance between Father and Son, in fact points in the opposite direction.

In her conclusion Pitstick insists that "Christ has come that we might *have life*, not death, and that we might have it in its fullness (see John 10:10). It would be the worst betrayal of this age (not to mention of Christ) to offer it elaborate theological platitudes suggesting its wounds *are* its life, thereby remaking God in its image" (p. 347). The characterization here of Balthasar's theology as platitudinous is surely rather polemical, but in other respects I would concur with Pitstick.

CHAPTER 6

Gender and "the Nuptial" in Balthasar's Theology

A discussion of gender has a natural place in an introduction to Balthasar, for his views on what it is to be "man" and "woman" are not just one topic among others in his writings, but flavor a great deal of his thought. What might be called the gendered character of his theology is one of the things that make him distinctive among modern theologians. Still more, however, an examination of gender has a natural place in a *critique* of Balthasar, for there is little in his thought that is such a flashpoint for controversy as what he has to say about women.

In what follows we will consider questions surrounding gender in two stages: we will first look at Balthasar's understanding of male and female taken in itself, and then turn to an examination of the role that this thinking plays in his theology more broadly. In some ways this is an artificial distinction, but it is nevertheless a useful one. Much of the critical reaction Balthasar's treatment of gender has attracted has been focused on what will here be the first stage — simply on what it is that he says about men and women, in particular about women — and this certainly merits consideration. But for my purposes it is what we will consider in the second stage, the role his understanding of man and woman plays in his theology as a whole, which is most important, for it is here that worries arise that are connected with the larger theme of this book.

Male and Female according to Balthasar

I have written of a critical reaction to Balthasar's views on gender, but it is important to be clear that not all the reaction is in fact critical. Some see Balthasar as laying the groundwork for an authentic Christian feminism,[1] or as pointing the way to a profound theology of otherness, bodiliness, and sexual difference. We will begin, then, by considering what might be taken as "selling points," aspects of his thought that supporters find important and appealing.

The first thing to say is simply that Balthasar does in fact take gender, and gender difference, seriously. Human beings do not exist apart from, independently of, their maleness or femaleness: we are not each an abstract individual, but specifically a man or a woman. This is something on which Balthasar is very forceful:

> The male body is male throughout, right down to each cell of which it consists and the female body is utterly female; and this is also true of their whole empirical experience and ego-consciousness. At the same time both share an identical human nature, but at no point does it protrude, neutrally, beyond the sexual difference, as if to provide a neutral ground for mutual understanding. Here there is no *universale ante rem,* as all theories of a nonsexual or bisexual (androgynous) primitive human being would like to think.[2]

Two of the things which contemporary intellectuals tend to think need more recognition — embodiment and difference — are (or seem to be) taken seriously here. First, we are not all the identical thinking beings,

1. Cf. Tina Beattie, *New Catholic Feminism: Theology and Theory* (London and New York: Routledge, 2006), esp. pp. 19-26, for a discussion of a "new Catholic feminism" which has emerged in recent years, and which draws on Balthasar as one of its chief sources. Beattie's book also contains one of the most robust and sustained critical treatments of Balthasar on gender and sexuality in print. Her approach is different from the one I am taking in this chapter; she describes her project as "a psycholinguistic probing of the underside of theological language and symbolism" (p. 8), and presents her book, in its style and structure, as a "parodic feminist staging of Hans Urs von Balthasar's idea of theo-drama" (p. 9).

2. *Theo-Drama,* Volume 2: *Dramatis Personae: Man in God,* trans. Graham Harrison (San Francisco: Ignatius Press, 1990), p. 364.

the autonomous intellects, envisaged by the Enlightenment, but are male or female, bodily creatures, living always as different to one another, and always in relation to one another.[3]

Second, Balthasar's characterization of women is not, prima facie at least, a negative one. Considerable portions of the Christian tradition have, for one reason or another, been tinged with misogyny: women have been thought, insofar as they are different from men, to be defective, inferior, or dangerous, and at times their gender has been seen as something they must transcend in order to attain sanctity. To all this, Balthasar's thought stands in sharp contrast. As we shall see in the next section, those traits or activities which he takes to be specifically female Balthasar seems to value highly, both as the appropriate mode of the creaturely response to God and of the Church to Christ (so that we must all become more "female" to be authentic Christians), and also as divine attributes, as ways in which in the eternal life of the Trinity God relates to God. Furthermore, the male is not on Balthasar's account seen as an autonomous, self-contained being, a pillar of strength or a model of full humanity, but rather as someone who is in some sense incomplete, very much in need of a woman for his fulfillment, for his having a home, for receiving a response, for the possibility of his own "fruitfulness." If the female is not (on the face of it at least) denigrated in Balthasar's thought, then also maleness as he depicts it is anything but "macho."[4]

3. It was necessary to add "or seem to be" in the previous sentence because on both counts (embodiment and difference) critics have raised questions. A number of thinkers have asked about whether the male-female difference that Balthasar describes is a *real* difference, as we shall see below. Tina Beattie also raises doubts about whether embodiment can really be said to be taken seriously in Balthasar's thought. After tracing the patterns of relationship one finds in Balthasar between Mary, the Church, and "woman," she concludes, "The maternal feminine *persona* in theo-drama, 'woman,' refers not to the sexual female body but primarily to the collective 'body' of the Church, and derivatively to the bodies of men who are women in relation to Christ" and then asks, "at this point . . . what has happened to the repeated insistence by Balthasar, the new feminists, and Pope John Paul II that an incarnational theology requires close attentiveness to the body's revelatory meaning? If the Church is woman, whose body does she feel with? Whose brain does she know with? Whose tongue does she speak with? Does she have breasts and a womb? Does she have a clitoris and a vagina?" (*New Catholic Feminism*, p. 108).

4. I am indebted to a comment of Francesca Murphy, in conversation, to the effect

Admirers of Balthasar on questions of gender might point to the relationship of his work to the thought (or experience) of Adrienne von Speyr as a lived confirmation of this last point. What other theologian of the twentieth century has been so profoundly influenced by a woman, and acknowledged that debt?[5] As we have seen, Balthasar described von Speyr's thought and his own as two halves of a single whole; he put tremendous effort into transcribing and publishing vast amounts of her work; and at her prompting he left the Society of Jesus and made himself, for the central period of his intellectual life, something of an ecclesial and theological outcast. All this would seem to point, one might argue, to the fact that Balthasar's positive valuation of the female was something real and fundamental, no mere intellectual posture.

What, then, precisely, does it mean, according to Balthasar, to be male or female? His most explicit discussions of gender difference (in both the second and the third volumes of the *Theo-Drama*) are based on his reading of (particularly the second of) the Genesis creation accounts, accounts which he takes to "embody much legendary wisdom on the part of mankind, purified of mythical bias" and to enable "an unprejudiced approach to the phenomenon [of sexuality]."[6] What we learn from Genesis, Balthasar thinks, is both the equality of the sexes and the primacy of the man. Man is primary, for "in this original situation he is alone before God and with God," but on the other hand "the man's (persisting) priority is located within an equality of man and woman."[7] We also learn that the man needs the woman for his fulfillment. Balthasar articulates this primarily in terms of a description of woman as *Antwort* and *Antlitz*, "answer" and "face." The woman is *Antwort* because "If man is the word that calls out, woman is the answer that comes to him at last,"[8] and *Antlitz* because "the man looks around and meets with an an-

---

that whatever else one might say of Balthasar, he is surely not a "macho" theologian. The point I am making here is slightly different, but clearly related.

5. I am grateful to my former student Aaron Riches for drawing my attention to the significance of this point.

6. *Man in God*, p. 368.

7. Ibid., p. 373.

8. *Theo-Drama*, Volume 3: *The Dramatis Personae: Persons in Christ*, trans. Graham Harrison (San Francisco: Ignatius, 1992), p. 284.

swering gaze."[9] Altogether, woman is both "man's delight" and "the help, the security, the home man needs . . . the vessel of fulfilment especially designed for him."[10]

Before going any further, it will be helpful to consider two questions, not at this stage for the purpose of criticism, but simply in order to be as clear as possible about the position Balthasar takes. First, how can it make sense to talk in the same breath of the equality of the sexes and the primacy of man? And secondly, how *asymetrically* ought we to interpret Balthasar's language of *Antwort* and *Antlitz,* and indeed of the woman as delight, help, security, home, fulfillment of the man? Might it be reasonable to suppose that all these things could also be said in reverse, so that man is also a response to woman, that he can also be the delight, home, security and fulfillment for her?

It will be helpful to begin with the second issue. Would it be possible to suppose that when Balthasar describes woman as in some way or other fulfilling and completing man, this is really shorthand for saying that each, in their difference, can be fulfillment, *Antwort* and *Antlitz,* for the other? Or to put it in a slightly different way, if it is the case, as Balthasar says, that the second account of creation shows that "the word that calls out only attains fulfillment when it is understood, accepted and given back as a word," could we deduce that the word which is given back (i.e., the woman's answer) also has the same requirements, that it too needs to be understood, accepted, and given back?

There is, in my judgment, a genuine ambiguity in Balthasar's thought on this point. One can indeed find passages to support the reading just outlined. In the context of talking about man and woman as *Litz* and *Antlitz,* for instance, Balthasar uses symmetrical, or nearly symmetrical, constructions: "Man and woman are face to face. . . . Man looks around him and meets with an answering gaze that turns the one-who-sees into the one-who-is-seen."[11] Each, it would seem, is equally faced with the other, and each plays the role both of the one seeing and the one seen. Or again, consider the following passage:

9. Ibid., p. 285.
10. Ibid.
11. Ibid.

127

As a human being, man is always in communion with his counter-image, woman, and yet never reaches her. The *converse is true of woman.* If we take this man/woman relationship as a paradigm, it also means that the human "I" is always searching for the "thou", and actually finds it ("This at last . . .") without ever being able to take possession of it in its otherness. Not only because the freedom of the "thou" cannot be mastered by the "I" using any superior transcendental grasp — since, in its proper context, all human freedom only opens up to absolute, divine freedom — but also because this impossibility is "enfleshed" in the diverse and complementary constitution of the sexes.[12]

Here, while sexual difference is insisted on, there is a clear sense of symmetry: each needs the other, each is an "I" in search of a "thou," each is the "counterimage" of the other. And one can find other passages which seem to point in the same direction, towards mutual need and mutual fulfillment.

Two points, however, militate against interpreting Balthasar's conception of sexual difference as a whole in light of such passages — against, that is to say, consistently interpreting Balthasar's language of woman as the fulfillment and completion of man as just a shorthand for the notion that each completes and fulfills the other. The first is that to be *Antwort* is presented as something like a *definition* of woman. "Woman as Answer" is the title of the section discussing male/female polarity in the third volume of the *Theo-Drama,* and Balthasar regularly reminds his reader, or sums up for his reader, what it means to be woman with a simple reference to "answer" or "answering." The second thing which prevents us from adopting such an interpretation is something to be discussed in more detail below, namely the way in which Balthasar consistently and insistently aligns the Christ/Church relationship with the male/female. There are elements of disanalogy, of course, between the archetypal Christ/Church relationship and that of Adam to Eve, man to woman, but one thing that is clearly not questioned is that in each case the second in the pairing comes after and answers, responds

12. *Man in God,* p. 366, emphasis added.

to, the first. An asymmetry between male and female, then, whereby the woman answers the man in a way that the man does not answer the woman, is lodged quite deeply in the structure of Balthasar's thought.

This brings us, then, back to our first question. What can it possibly mean in such a context to speak of equality between the sexes? As we have already seen, Balthasar takes the second account of creation in Genesis to indicate that "the word that calls out only attains fulfillment when it is understood, accepted and given back as a word." He goes on to say, "This clearly shows us the way in which man can be primary and woman secondary, where the primary remains unfulfilled without the secondary. *The primary needs a partner of equal rank and dignity for its own fulfillment.*"[13] One way to reconcile what Balthasar says about primacy and what he says about equality, then (if we are not to take it simply as a mystery), is this: if the woman's role is to provide the man with the response he needs, in order to do this she must be on a level with him, "flesh of his flesh," not just yet one more inferior animal. She may be ordered to him in a way that he is not to her — her function may revolve around what she can do for him in a way that his does not revolve around her — but if she is to *fulfill* this function, she needs to be on a level with him.

While, as I have said, Balthasar's most explicit discussions of the nature of man and woman are offered in relation to Genesis, for a full picture of the way he understands gender difference one needs to look further. Scattered throughout many of Balthasar's writings are references, often brief and in passing, almost always unargued, to what it is to be a man, or what womanliness is. From a broader reading, then, one can come up with a list something like this: to be male is to be strong, to take initiative, to be active and goal-orientated; to be woman is to be open, receptive, surrendering, passive, to be characterized by weakness and dependence, to be contemplative. And within these clusters, perhaps the most insistent, frequently mentioned, the defining contrast, is that man takes initiative and is active, while woman is receptive.

How does Balthasar know all this? How does he know, for instance, that to be male is to be active, to be a woman is to be receptive? Where does he learn this? One might try to construe this as a kind of extension of

13. *Persons in Christ*, p. 284, emphasis added.

what was already discussed in connection with Genesis, of male primacy and the answering role of woman. But if one looks at the Genesis stories themselves it is in fact rather hard to see how one could claim to learn of male activity and female receptivity from them. Indeed, if one were to insist that there is something to be learned about activity and receptivity from them, the Adam and Eve narratives would seem to point in quite the opposite direction from the one Balthasar takes.[14] Fundamentally, these characteristics seem rather to be read off of the respective male and female roles in sexual intercourse, or more precisely, as Fergus Kerr puts it, "all very much on analogy with male/female sexual coupling, as traditionally conceived."[15] The centrality of the sexual act to Balthasar's thought about gender is something to which we will be returning below.

Balthasar's presentation of gender, considered in itself, can give rise to a range of concerns. A criticism which has been voiced from more than one quarter is that while Balthasar appears to insist on and make much of sexual difference, it is not a *real* sexual difference that he envisages, but one which begins from man and then casts woman as whatever is needed to complement and fulfill him. He is trapped, it has been argued, in a "one-sex" anthropology, "in which the normative human being is implicitly male and Woman's definition is based around Man, particularly around what Man is seen to need Woman to be."[16]

Another issue, and one we have already begun to touch on, is how seriously one can take Balthasar's championing of the equality of the sexes, sitting as it does alongside, on the one hand, his characterization of women in terms of weakness, dependence, and surrender, and on the other hand, his insistence on male primacy.

I suggested above a way of reconciling Balthasar's affirmation of

---

14. Cf. Phyllis Trible's "Eve and Adam: Genesis 2–3 Reread," *Andover Newton Quarterly* 13 (1973): 77-81, which includes the somewhat tongue-in-cheek suggestion that the woman's being the first to take the fruit from the serpent is part of the story's portrayal of Eve as a person of initiative, over-against a rather passive Adam.

15. *Twentieth-Century Catholic Theologians* (Oxford: Blackwell, 2007), p. 143.

16. Corinne Crammer, "One Sex or Two?: Balthasar's Theology of the Sexes," in *The Cambridge Companion to Hans Urs von Balthasar*, ed. Edward T. Oakes, S.J., and David Moss (Cambridge: Cambridge University Press, 2004), p. 102. Crammer goes on to add that "Woman in Balthasar's theology lacks substance, subjectivity, and a voice of her own." Similar points have been made by Gerard Loughlin, Tina Beattie, and Ben Quash.

male primacy with his insistence on equality between the sexes: woman is ordered to man, she is created for the sake of and for the needs of man, and in order to *fulfill* these needs, she must be an equal (i.e., flesh of his flesh, a human being). This is a solution which will not, however, set everyone at ease. To put the difficulty in a Kantian idiom, Balthasar would seem to be suggesting that man is (relatively speaking, at least, within the created order)[17] an end in himself, whereas woman is not.

And how can one speak of equality of the sexes while describing women in terms of weakness, dependence, and surrender? A defender might respond that it is a mistake (perhaps a classic mistake of a male-oriented modernity) to think of these qualities negatively, to think that these make one inferior, that they are less valuable than initiative, strength, action, and so on. For these "weak" characteristics are in fact what is fundamental to us all in our relation to God, and these qualities are found even within the life of God (as we shall see in the next section). If anything, one might say, Balthasar is portraying women as ahead of the game, having the edge over the men, precisely in this weakness, dependence, and surrender.

Can one be satisfied by such a response? I think the answer has to be "no." Certainly, in relation to God, weakness, dependence, and surrender on the part of the creature can be construed in positive terms. But there is no question — nor should there be — of equality between God and creature. To speak of these characteristics as fundamentally *womanly*, however, is, in the first instance at least, to see them not in relation to God but in relation to men. A notion of *mutual* dependence and mutual surrender would of course be reconcilable with equality, but Balthasar very specifically aligns womanliness (and not masculinity) with weakness, surrender, and dependence. Fundamentally, Balthasar's logic is that women relate to men in something of the way all should relate to God, and whatever else we make of this, conducive to the notion of equality between men and women it is not.[18]

---

17. I add this qualification to forestall the reply that we are in fact *all* for the sake of something beyond ourselves, for the sake of Christ, or of God. This may be true, but as Balthasar presents the matter, women nevertheless exist, within the creaturely sphere, for the sake of men in a way that men do not exist for the sake of women.

18. Doubts about the seriousness with which Balthasar can affirm equality between

Another issue is Balthasar's persistent alignment of the male/female distinction with a contrast between activity and receptivity. Again, defenders of Balthasar would be keen to point out that this does not involve any denigration of the female — both because it is an *active* receptivity he discusses, not a mere passivity, and because receptivity is something genuinely positive, the highest vocation of all human beings and indeed an aspect of the divine life. But again this is not necessarily entirely reassuring: it is hard not to sense a kind of trap in the thoroughgoing identification of the female with receptivity, no matter how positively the latter is conceived. More than one commentator has pointed out an interesting asymmetry in Balthasar's thought: men, while fundamentally active, are able also to be female and receptive, but women cannot in turn also be active.[19]

And even if we set all this aside, there is the question of how *plausible* it is, from any perspective, to identify women so fundamentally with receptivity. Even if one has no qualms about ascribing an "essential" nature to women,[20] and even if one thinks that such a nature is more or less accurately reflected in the traditional woman's role in our culture, there remain problems. Suppose I like to bake cakes: this would make me, in one respect at least, stereotypically female — but not in fact particularly receptive. Indeed, having baked the cakes, I may well like to have people to whom I can *give* them. The example is flippant, but a great array of traditional female roles — cooking, cleaning, feeding, organizing the home — are active, and are very much to do with giving rather than receiving.[21] The notion of women as receptive is derived from the (traditionally conceived) act of in-

---

men and women might find some support from the fact that in his relatively early collection of aphorisms, *The Grain of Wheat*, Balthasar at one stage straightforwardly presumes a God-willed male superiority. The context is an aphorism on homosexuality, which is "so ruinous because here man has caught sight of his own beauty and made it into an object. If the male is involved, he has likewise objectivized his God-willed superiority" (p. 88).

19. Men can be "female" and receptive as Christians, in relation to God, but women cannot take on the fundamentally active and male role of the priesthood.

20. Cf. Serene Jones's *Feminist Theory and Christian Theology* (Minneapolis: Fortress, 2000) for a helpful discussion of essentialism and constructivism in a theological context.

21. I am of course using "traditional" here in a very limited sense. If we look a bit further, traditional female roles ought to include, for instance, growing the crops, which again is not particularly receptive.

tercourse, and has perhaps also a certain fit with traditional courting patterns, but can find little purchase in relation to the great majority of the roles women currently do play or have traditionally played.

But perhaps, one could respond to all this, a sensible person might have guessed in advance that if examining a Swiss theologian of patrician background educated in the early part of the twentieth century, one might not find ideas about gender or sexuality that will exactly match our own, that will seem to most of us either wholly attractive or wholly persuasive. Balthasar was no doubt in certain respects at least a man of his time, and if we are searching for illumination about gender, one might say, this is just not the place to look.

What is most striking about Balthasar's views on gender, however, is not really that they are, or seem to many, less than satisfactory, but that they are so pervasive to his theology, that they saturate so much of his thinking. In his case it cannot be, then, as it may well be in others, that on this issue there is a little pocket in his thought that we may judge has not aged so well, and would do better to avoid. One can hardly, in fact, turn a corner in Balthasar's thought without running into gender, and the relations between men and women. And it is to this phenomenon, and what to make of it, that we now turn.

Male and Female Put to Work Theologically

We have inevitably already touched at some points on the theological role of gender in Balthasar's thought, but a convenient place to begin a more sustained consideration of it is with the essay "Who Is the Church?" in the second volume of his *Theological Explorations*. The question Balthasar asks here is whether the Church is a person, not just in the way that a nation might be spoken of as a kind of collective person, but in some real sense; and, if so, then who this person is. It is not, then, an essay *about* gender, but it is one which turns out to provide a rich sampling of Balthasar's *use* of gendered categories.[22]

22. For a careful study of this essay from the point of view of its biblical exegesis, cf. W. T. Dickens's *Hans Urs von Balthasar's* Theological Aesthetics: *A Model for Post-Critical*

A theme that emerges strongly is that Balthasar wants to bring the language of Ephesians of the Church as the Bride of Christ, and so a male/female relation between Christ and the Church, to the center of ecclesiological reflection. This image of the Church had been lost, or at least blurred, during the Counter-Reformation, in favor of a hierarchical and institutional conception of the Church, and in more recent theology it is the analogy of the body which has dominated. In the context of this essay, and the question of *who* the Church is, the Bride image is important, for it involves presenting the Church as a person in some sense in her own right, a second subject or agent in relation to Christ, rather than simply a kind of extension of Christ. One of the central discussions of the essay is in fact over the question of how to relate what one might call the *over-againstness* of Christ and Church involved in the image of bride and bridegroom, with the *identification* suggested in the language of the Church as Christ's body.

What is interesting to observe, however, is the way the language of bride and bridegroom is in fact extended in several directions beyond the biblical starting point relating to Christ and Church. First of all, Balthsaar also freely writes of *individual* Christians as in a marital relation to God. Thus we read, for instance, "The encounter that, at its maximum intensity, merits the name of marriage is personal and takes place between God as person and man as person,"[23] or again, that even if Church structures and sacraments are provisional, "What never falls away is the nuptial encounter between God and the creature."[24] Second, Balthasar writes

---

Biblical Interpretation (Notre Dame: University of Notre Dame Press, 2003), ch. 5, pp. 207-33. Dickens concludes that in a number of ways Balthasar's exegetical practice here both violates his own hermeneutical principles and "part[s] ways with the reigning historical critical consensus" (p. 220), but that it is best viewed as an example of "performance interpretation," a notion he derives from Nicholas Lash and John Riches. Dickens, it should be noted, focuses primarily on Balthasar's identification of the Church, as bride of Christ, with Mary.

23. "Who Is the Church?" in *Explorations in Theology,* Volume 2: *Spouse of the Word,* trans. A. V. Littledale (San Francisco: Ignatius, 1991), p. 157.

24. Ibid., p. 158. Balthasar also writes of "the individual believer [who] lets himself be taken by God" (p. 188); it is clear from the context here, I should add, that "being taken" has a distinctly gendered connotation (so, for instance at another point, and in relation to "feminine dependence on God" Balthasar writes of there being, with God, "no taking but only a being taken").

of *Mary* as bride of Christ, and this needs to be considered, not just as one more example of an individual in a nuptial relation with God, but as a key principle in its own right. It is because "the Lord wills to see his Church standing before him, not as a singular, palpable failure but as a glorious bride worthy of him" that Mary is so crucial: "Mary is the subjectivity that, in its womanly and receptive manner, is enabled fully to correspond to the masculine subjectivity of Christ, through God's grace and overshadowing of his Spirit."[25] Third, the masculine/feminine imagery of Christ and Church is extended to describe relations within the Church, between the official, hierarchical element of the Church and the laity. So, for instance, we read that "the office and the Sacrament are forms of communicating the seed; they belong to the male aspect, but their end is to lead the bride to her womanly function and fortify her in it," or again that "the representative of 'office' has the masculine function of the one who gives, and the 'laity' the feminine one of receiving."[26] And finally, there is at least a hint here that the masculine/feminine imagery in relation to Christ and Church is extendable into the Trinity. Thus at one point, in the context of an exploration of the analogy between the Church's coming into being and "the marriage act," Balthasar writes:

> For the Church to come into being, a productive act is required, and this extends from the Man dying on the Cross (who lets body and spirit and person flow out of himself so fully that he is himself all outpouring and seed, that the Creator dissolves in the creation, the priest in the sacrifice) — extends through the communication of his own both human and divine spirit into the very mysteries of the generation and spiration within the Trinity. Here indeed the person is not distinguished from the life flow in which the Father is active generation, the Son passive generation.[27]

There is thus a linking intended here between the activity of the Trinity and the "generative" activity of Jesus on the Cross, itself linked analogously

25. Ibid., p. 161.
26. Ibid., p. 158.
27. Ibid., p. 188.

to sexual activity. If it is not entirely clear here whether the language of the Father as active generation and the Son as passive is intended to suggest an alignment between the Father and masculinity and the Son and femininity, this is something which elsewhere is considerably less ambiguous. In the fifth volume of *Theo-Drama,* for instance, Balthasar writes that "In trinitarian terms, of course, the Father, who begets him who is without origin, appears primarily as (super-)masculine; the Son, in consenting, appears initially as (super-)feminine."[28] There is no question, perhaps, of any really *simple* sexual division, since, in relation to the breathing forth of the Spirit, Balthasar says, the Son is "(super-)masculine" and indeed "There is even something (super-)feminine about the Father too, since, as we have shown, in the action of begetting and breathing forth he allows himself to be determined by the Persons who thus proceed from him"[29] — but Balthasar is confident here and at other points that *some* kind of gendered language is appropriately used of the Trinity.

A second thing to notice in this essay — and this is something very often true in Balthasar's theology more broadly — is how focused around *sexual intercourse* Balthasar's gendered imagery is. Much of it is of course, as we have seen, a kind of extension of the image of the Church as bride of Christ, but Balthasar has a tendency to interpret the image of bride and bridegroom in a strikingly concrete and biologically specific way. Consider, for instance, an example of his discussion of the role of the official and sacramental side of the Church in relation to the laity:

> The bride is essentially woman, that is, receptive: one who, through acceptance of the seed but also through all her own female organs and powers is made competent to bring forth and bear fruit. In bringing forth at birth (which, in a broad sense, includes her care of the child and his feeding and upbringing to full independence), woman gives to man the complete, superabundant response. . . . The office and the Sacrament are forms of communicating the seed: they belong to the

28. *Theo-Drama,* Volume 5: *The Last Act,* trans. Graham Harrison (San Francisco: Ignatius, 1998), p. 91.
29. Ibid.

male aspect, but their end is to lead the bride to her womanly function and fortify her in it. Part of this, indeed, is her ability to receive a supernatural seed, an ability that itself is capable of development from a low to a high potential; and it includes, besides, the power to preserve the seed, to make it bring forth much fruit in the "good ground," a hundred-, sixty-, and thirty-fold (Matt. 15:8-9).[30]

We see here not just some general reference to marriage as love and union, but a quite concretely imagined pattern of a male party inseminating a female party, who in turn bears the seed and brings forth (and then feeds and raises) a child from that seed. And Balthasar gives not only very concretely worked out descriptions of what it means to be bride of Christ, in terms of a "passive reception" which is, fundamentally, "the female activity of seed bearing, giving birth, and educating," but also arrestingly sexual conceptions of Christ as bridegroom: we have already seen a reference to the "productive act" of Christ on the Cross, "who lets body and spirit and person flow out of himself so fully that he is himself all outpouring and seed," but one can also read of the Eucharist as an extension of this same pattern: "What else is his eucharist but, at a higher level, an endless act of fruitful outpouring of his whole flesh, such as a man can only achieve for a moment with a limited organ of his own body."[31]

Even when seeds and wombs and male outpourings do not specifically appear in Balthasar's writings, it is often still clear that the underly-

---

30. "Who Is the Church?," p. 158.

31. *Elucidations*, p. 226. Tina Beattie writes, not without some justification, that "Balthasar's theology oozes sex" (157). Corinne Crammer, similarly, notes that "Although Balthasar is at pains to reject sexuality or sexual difference as we know it in the Trinity, nevertheless, his description of divine activities at times sounds vividly reminiscent of sexual reproduction: the divine Persons penetrate each other. The Holy Spirit is the fruit of the love between the Father and the Son, who together generate the Spirit in an act of communal love. Christ's giving away of himself in the Eucharist [as we have seen] is compared to a man having intercourse, and in the act of procreation, a man 'represents only a distant analogy to this Trinitarian and christological event' of the generation of the Son.... God's kenotic love empties itself out into Mary's womb as an infinitesimally small seed in order to let the God-bearer ripen it and bring it into the world" ("One Sex or Two?" p. 101).

ing logic has a good deal to do with sexual intercourse. Thus, for instance, we find Balthasar asserting that while the man's fruitfulness is "primary," the woman too has a fruitfulness, "an answering fruitfulness, designed to receive man's fruitfulness (which, in itself, is helpless) and bring it to its 'fullness.'"[32] Or again, the woman "receive[s] man's fruitfulness into her own fruitfulness, thus uniting in herself the fruitfulness of both."[33] It is hard to know how to understand such passages except in terms of sexual reproduction.

Balthasar uses the word "nuptial" quite often, and some of those influenced by him even more so.[34] In its haziness, however, this term is in danger of misleading. "Nuptial" is an adjective for things related to weddings, or to marriages. Weddings, in the gospels and elsewhere, have much to do with ceremonies, with eating and drinking, bridesmaids, family tensions, and so on, and marriages with permanent public commitment, with the running of households, the linking of families, the sharing of property, the (shared) project of raising children,[35] the general business of leading life together. None of these, however, is ever even in the background when Balthasar refers to brides, bridegrooms, and nuptiality. On the whole this dimension in Balthasar's thought could more accurately, if perhaps less politely, be described as pointing towards a sexual-intercourse theology than a nuptial one.

There is, to put this point another way, a kind of sexual reductionism to be felt in Balthasar's theological use of gender imagery. And it is not only that male/female relationships are all conceived as marital, and that marriage is considered entirely in terms of sex; sexuality itself, here, is reduced to a sort of biologically conceived act of reproduction. We read much, in Balthasar, as we have seen, of seeds and wombs and gestation periods, but we in fact hear very little of erotic love. He does, as we have seen, use the language of male giving and female receiving, but on

---

32. *Persons in Christ*, p. 226.

33. Ibid., p. 286.

34. Cf. for instance Angelo Scola's *The Nuptial Mystery* (Grand Rapids: Eerdmans, 2005).

35. As we have seen, the bearing and raising of a child is a part of Balthasar's concept of nuptiality, but it is always only one child, and consistently construed as, after the point of insemination, almost entirely the mother's doing.

neither side (rather surprisingly, in view of the tradition) is there any consistent mention of beauty,[36] or allure, or *desire*. To put it another way, though Balthasar mentions the Song of Solomon in the context of arguing for the biblical importance of "nuptiality," few echoes of the Song, or of the tradition's mystical reading of it, are in fact to be heard in his thought. It is sexual reproduction, rather than sexual love, that seems to govern Balthasar's "nuptial" thought.[37]

One might ask *why* gender and the "nuptial" are so very prominent in Balthasar's theology. We could point to the influence of Henri de Lubac, and beyond that to the influence of Origen on both de Lubac and Balthasar, but this is not enough to account either for the particular *shape* the nuptial takes, as we have seen, in Balthasar, nor for the striking prominence it has. Could there be a psychological explanation?[38] Could it be, consciously or unconsciously, a Catholic theological response to broader cultural developments (feminism, the sexual revolution)? Might there be ecclesial-political considerations behind all this, having to do with the need to have a deep theological justification for the non-ordination of women?[39] Or might the attractiveness of gender and the "nuptial" lie simply in the way it allows Balthasar to hold together divine and created agency? If one says that God is always male in relation to a female creation, and understands male and female as Balthasar does, then it becomes possible to conceive of the divine as that which always takes the initiative, without which the creature is completely helpless, and yet to affirm a genuine creaturely fruitfulness: just as the woman, in sexual intercourse traditionally imagined, cannot do anything on her own, and cannot initiate, but is entirely dependent on the prior activity of the man, so the creature can only respond to a divine initiative. But

---

36. Beauty, of course, as we have seen in Chapter Three, is a major topic for Balthasar, but it is not particularly central in the *nuptial* aspect of his thought.

37. Cf. Tina Beattie's *New Catholic Feminism,* pp. 117-20, for an overview of the contrasting ways Balthasar and Gregory of Nyssa handle nuptial symbolism.

38. For a psycho-analytic approach, see Tina Beattie's discussion of Balthasar's relationship with Adrienne von Speyr in *New Catholic Feminism.*

39. I would myself find it implausible to account for this whole dimension of Balthasar's theology in these terms, although perhaps not so implausible to account for the attractiveness of Balthasar's "nuptial" theology to *others* at least partly in these terms.

just as the woman, having received the seed, genuinely does something with it — she brings it to fruition as a child — so the creature really does bring forth something of its own in response to God's grace.[40]

Whatever the reasons, it is clear that in Balthasar's thought "the nuptial" is not just one metaphor among others, but a uniquely privileged one. But is this not, one might ask, simply Balthasar being a good Catholic theologian? Does he not privilege this metaphor because it is biblical, and if he goes beyond the original biblical context, for instance, in speaking of Mary as bride of Christ, is he not simply following tradition? In fact, I want to suggest, in the way he deploys the nuptial metaphor Balthasar stands above both Scripture and tradition, weaving the materials he finds in them into a pattern which is very much his own.

It is undeniable, of course, that one finds spousal imagery in Old Testament treatments of Israel's relation to its Lord, and that in New Testament texts we find not only reference to the Church as "bride of Christ" but something of a sustained analogy between the male/female marital relation and the Christ/Church relationship. But there is other imagery to be found in the Old Testament (God as judge or king, for example) and there are other images employed to describe the relation of his followers to Christ in the New Testament: servants, brothers, and friends make an appearance at least as often as brides, and if we leave behind the sphere of the interpersonal, then there is the relationship of sheep to shepherd, branches to vine, even perhaps of seed to farmer (as well, of course, as the much used body/head image). Two things are striking in Balthasar's handling of this range of imagery. The first is simply that he so often singles out one form of interpersonal relationship above all others: the spousal relationship displaces all other kinds of kinship (i.e., between siblings, between father and son, mother and child)[41] and also displaces

---

40. One might also, of course, *criticize* this use of gender imagery for placing divine and human agency too much on the same plane. The male/female structuring allows for something like a "division of labor" between God and creature (God has the male role, the creature the female) which in turn suggests a possibility of competition between divine and created agency. Cf. Kathryn Tanner's *God and Creation in Christian Theology: Tyranny or Empowerment?* (Oxford: Basil Blackwell, 1988) for an argument about the centrality to the Christian tradition of a *non-contrastive* conception of divine and created agency.

41. Cf. Janet Soskice's *The Kindness of God* (Oxford: Oxford University Press, 1998) for a

friendship, to become *the* way of framing interpersonal intimacy in the Christ-Church and God-creature relationship. Equally striking is the way in which a number of other central New Testament images (the sowing of seeds, the bearing of fruit) are removed from their original agricultural setting in relation to grain and grape and absorbed into a sexual scheme; the "fruitfulness" of the Christian in relation to Christ calls to mind, in Balthasar's usage, no longer an image of a branch in its dependence on the vine, bringing forth grapes, but instead an image of a woman who bears "fruit," i.e., a child, from the "seed" of the man.[42]

Particularly revealing of Balthasar's stance in relation to Scripture are his comments on portions of the canon which do *not* frame the Christ-Church or God-creature relationship in sexual imagery. In the Song of Songs, for instance, while there is of course sexual imagery, the fact that there is "never even a hint of reference to the relations between Yahweh and Israel" Balthasar terms "an amazing piece of *discretion.*"[43] He finds this same "discretion" in the few synoptic texts where, though weddings and bridegrooms are mentioned, it is not clear that the bridegroom is to be identified with Christ himself, and the bride is not identified at all.[44] Balthasar's treatment of the Gospel of John (and of Revelation, which he ascribes to the same author) is especially interesting. Here we see him again characterizing this lack of reference to a marital relationship between Christ and Church as a kind of intentional holding back, a deliber-

---

broad-ranging exploration of the importance of kinship metaphors in thinking about the God-creature relationship.

42. Some have seen — and praised — in Balthasar a style of scriptural interpretation alien to modern historical-critical sensibilities but close to that of the Church Fathers, a style which involves, within a broad Christological framing, a certain spontaneity and fluidity of movement among biblical texts. What we have seen here, however, is not so much an enriching creativity of association between scriptural motifs as the systematic subordination of a range of metaphors and images to a single controlling theme.

43. "Who Is the Church?," p. 152, emphasis added.

44. "It is difficult to assess, in this context, the import of the few *synoptic texts* that bridge the gap between the nuptial theology of the prophets and that of Paul. What stands out, here also, is their *discretion,* which goes so far that it is always doubtful whether Jesus was describing himself as a Bridegroom of the new redeemed community or was merely adopting the nuptial simile as the traditional image of the messianic era." Ibid, p. 151, emphasis added.

ate silence, but at the same time fusing a variety of other images and motifs into something which turns out to be sexual. So, on the one hand, he describes John as being "always *more reserved* than the prophets" and "*as silent* as the other evangelists on the personal character of the bride Church."[45] On the other hand, while it may be that the reference to bride and bridegroom[46] does not, considered in itself, "point to anything beyond the messianic connection,"[47] Balthasar suggests that if one takes these words "as part of the general content and significance of the Gospel," they do point to something more. He lists a whole series of elements in the gospel that express intimacy between Christ and his followers and have a fleshly, bodily dimension, and then seems to suggest that these all, cumulatively, indicate a nuptial relation between Christ and the Church.[48]

What I would like to suggest here is not that Balthasar's exegesis is flawed, that it is not as careful or balanced or persuasive as it might be, but rather that exegesis as usually conceived is simply not the best way to understand what he is engaged in. The commentary Balthasar offers on biblical texts does not make sense if one tries to detect in it an argu-

45. Ibid., pp. 153, 152, emphasis added.

46. "He who has the bride is the bridegroom. The friend of the bridegroom, who stands and hears him, rejoices greatly at the bridegroom's voice" (John 3:29).

47. "Who Is the Church?," p. 152.

48. It is a little difficult to analyze Balthasar's argument closely here, in part because it is so very sketchy. He indicates the "general context and significance of the Gospel," for instance, simply by offering a list of motifs, free of any commentary: "the Word being made flesh (1:14); the marriage feast at Cana (2:1-11); the 'temple of his body' (2:21); the return to the womb in order to be reborn (3:4); the giving of his flesh and blood for the life of the world (6:33f.); the fountain of living water flowing from him (7:37-38); his freely giving his life for his sheep (10:17); the royal entry of the 'daughter of Zion' (12:15); the vine and its branches (15:1-8); his giving his mother to the disciple (19:27); the opening of his side (19:34); the breathing of the Holy Spirit (20:22); the hand in the wound (20:27); and, the outcome of all this, the designation of the Church as 'the elect lady and her children' (2 John 1) and the eschatological vision of the spouse of the Lamb (Rev. 21:22)" (p. 152). From all this he concludes that "the relation between Christ and the Church goes far beyond that between Yahweh and Israel" and that a "far more intimate relationship has been created and communicated through Christ's bodily nature, one transcending even that conveyed in the nuptial image of the Letter to the Ephesians, though including it" (p. 152). The content of the whole discussion makes it clear that this "intimacy," while it may transcend the *particular* nuptial image of Ephesians, is still nevertheless to be interpreted nuptially.

ment *from* these texts *to* a nuptial understanding of Christ and Church, God and creation. A far more coherent reading becomes possible if one takes the movement to be in the opposite direction: from the standpoint of an *already given* nuptial scheme Balthasar offers a wide-ranging survey and explanation of biblical texts. In this light one can begin to understand the fusion he engages in of different strands of biblical imagery, including the subordination of various kinds of metaphor to the sexual. If we already know that the *deepest* understanding of the relationship of Christ to the Church is a sexual one, then of course it may be fitting to read the biblical language of fruits and vines, or of the planting and harvesting of grain, through the lens of male/female relations. Indeed, unless Balthasar is surveying Scripture in light of an already presumed nuptial scheme, how could he be in a position to suggest that the *absence* of the nuptial scheme from, for instance, all of the gospels is to be read as a matter of "discretion" and "reserve" — i.e., to suggest, as such terms do, that ultimately these texts (or their authors) have something in mind about which they *choose* to remain silent?[49]

49. In a rather different context, John Riches reaches a similar conclusion about the relationship between Balthasar's distinctive theological commitments and his approach to Scripture. In "Von Balthasar as Biblical Theologian and Exegete" in *New Blackfriars* 79 (1998): 38-45, Riches focuses particularly on Balthasar's treatment of the New Testament in the final volume of *The Glory of the Lord*. He traces the pattern familiar to us from Chapter Four, above: according to Balthasar Scripture "is not the centre of the revelation *Gestalt*" but the "the interpretive reflection on and circling around that mystery.... The centre is something that can be reached only through that which is mediated, derivative." Contrary to what one might expect, Riches notes, Balthasar does not therefore "allow the New Testament writings to mediate to him the central *Gestalt*, and then offer his own readings as further mediations of that central reality.... Instead, surprisingly, he offers his own reconstruction of the revelation figure of the Word made flesh, and places it *before* the section in which he treats of the New Testament writings' account of glory." The result is that Balthasar's "highly idiosyncratic vision of the *triduum mortis* ... controls his whole subsequent reading of the canon, indeed that *it assumes pride of place over the canon*" (p. 41, emphasis added).

Riches's approach to Balthasar is broadly positive: there is much that he describes as "liberative" in Balthasar's theology; he sees the latter's reconstruction of the central *Gestalt* of revelation as "deeply moving," and thinks that it can be "instructive and fruitful" in the way that other church theology can be. The worry Riches raises, however, is that

Something similar can be said about the way Balthasar responds to tradition. It is true, of course, that in his interest in gender and sex Balthasar takes up certain traditional themes. One can find in the writings of the mystics a basis for construing individual union with God in sexual terms, and in medieval theology precedent for speaking of Mary as the bride of Christ. And yet Balthasar's procedure is not so much one of simply learning from or following tradition, as it is drawing out those elements from tradition which, perhaps after some modification, fit with and illustrate an already established nuptial scheme. He is engaged in systematizing a variety of traditional themes, melding them, and extending them, into a single pattern, so that what had previously been individual metaphors, motifs, or ideas, developed here or there in the history of theology and spirituality, become in his presentation (and even more clearly in that of some of his followers) interlinked components of an overarching system.

That Balthasar is arguing *from* his nuptial scheme rather than *to* it in relation to tradition (as in relation to the Bible) can be seen from the kinds of judgments he makes about various moments of the tradition. Consider, for instance, his treatment of the historical development of Mariology. Balthasar here offers a narrative in which it is made clear to the reader which new ideas and motifs represent progress, authentic development, and which are unfortunate deviation. The high Middle Ages, for instance, he considers to be a time of "breakthrough," when something fundamentally important was clearly recognized, and also a time of distortion. The "breakthrough" happened, he suggests, "in the twelfth century, when the Song of Songs was understood to refer to Mary not only in individual verses . . . but in its totality,"[50] and so it seems, the notion that Mary is bride of Christ was clearly affirmed. But this new insight, Balthasar thinks, could also be taken too far: "the Bride-Bridegroom theology and the rhetorical forms resulting from it can adopt highly dubious, sensual connotations: Mary is seen as Christ's lover; her beauty is such that she entrances God and 'entices' him to become man!"[51] He proposes then to

---

Balthasar in effect turns "what is an imaginative and creative theological meditation into something which looks as if it is canonical" (p. 43).

50. *Persons in Christ*, p. 309.

51. Ibid.

turn his and the reader's attention "not to these exaggerations, but to the legitimate 'summing up' of the Church's attributes in Mary, in whom alone the whole idea of the Church is realized." One aspect of the theology of the time is legitimate, another dubious, exaggerated. What is the principle by which one decides which is which? The criteria are distinctly underdeveloped in Balthasar's presentation. There are hints, at least, of why he rejects what he chooses to reject: some developments are too sensual, and some infringe on the status of Christ, or on the creature/creator distinction. By why does he approve of that which he approves? Here, for the most part, no reasons are given at all. That it is proper and important to term Mary the bride of Christ, in other words, is presumed by his treatment of tradition, rather than established by it.

The sense that Balthasar is sifting the tradition in light of an established scheme continues right through to the final stage of his discussion of the history of Mariology, i.e., to his treatment of the Second Vatican Council. This most recent phase of the tradition falls under criticism from Balthasar, not for dubious exaggeration, but for not saying enough. Balthasar grants that the Council's Mariology is "based on Scripture and the main lines pursued by the Fathers" but criticizes it for "fail[ing] to give attention to a number of themes that, while developed at a later stage, *seem essential.*"[52] How one determines that themes developed at a certain point are essential, and so chides one stage in the tradition for not repeating the themes of another, is not specified explicitly. Balthasar's criticism of the Council for the introduction of an "over-cautious" citation from Ambrose, however, may provide a clue. Ambrose is cited to the effect that "Mary's cooperation does not add anything . . . to the work of Christ, the one Mediator";[53] the problem with this is that while it may "[do] justice to the relationship between God, the sole source of grace, and the creature," it fails to "give full weight to *the man-woman aspect.*"[54] That there *must be* a significant "man-woman aspect" to the Church's reflection on Mary in relation to Christ, in other words, is the norm by which the tradition is sifted and judged.

52. Ibid., p. 317, emphasis added.
53. Ibid., p. 318.
54. Ibid., emphasis added.

Summary

There are a whole range of ways in which one might want to question Balthasar's construal of sex and the genders, as well as what one might call his gendering and sexualizing of theology. Is woman really dual in contrast to a more unified man? Can women be both secondary and equal to men? Are they really more contemplative? Is there something intrinsically "male" about the clergy in relation to a "female" laity? Ought Cross and Eucharist to be construed in sexual terms? Should we retrieve the notion of Mary as bride of her son? Ought we to consider the second person of the Trinity female in relation to the first?

In the context of the larger theme of this book, however, what I am attempting to draw attention to is not really individual difficulties or contestable judgments, but the whole pattern, the shape, of Balthasar's thought on gender. Of concern is not so much the plausibility of specific claims, then, but the fact that an understanding of gender and sex for which Balthasar nowhere offers significant arguments (the discussion of Genesis provides ultimately an illustration of his position rather than a warrant for it) informs and shapes Balthasar's anthropology, Mariology, ecclesiology, doctrine of the Trinity, and so on. Gender and sexuality become for Balthasar something of a framework uniting many of the loci of theology, a key in light of which Scripture is organized and interpreted, a norm by which tradition is sifted. Gender is not, of course, the *sole* concern or the only source of his theology, but it is a major theme, and beyond this it illuminates the kind of stance Balthasar takes in relation to his material. He writes as someone who already knows — without ever specifying how he knows — what are the deepest truths in relation to gender, and who already knows, without again ever really needing to make a case for this — how gender and sex lie at the heart of a range of theological issues, and as someone who can then expound Scripture, tradition, and dogma to us in light of this already known inner structure.

CHAPTER 7

Conclusion

Fergus Kerr concludes a chapter on Balthasar in his *Twentieth-Century Catholic Theologians* with the following sentence:

> He is by far the most discussed Catholic theologian at present, as the ever-expanding secondary literature shows, overwhelmingly positive in tenor, which is perhaps surprising — unless critics do not know where to start.[1]

The problem of where to start if one wants to criticize Balthasar is, I think, a real one, for reasons sketched in the introductory chapter: the vast sweep of Balthasar's writings; the lack of any clear organizing center; the sheer range of his reference; the predominance of description over argument; and so on. What is most problematic in Balthasar, I have suggested, is no one bit of his thought, no one theological position, no separately extractable methodological principle, but something pervading the whole, or nearly the whole, of his work, something about the mode of his theology, something which can be articulated in terms of the theological "voice" of Balthasar, and the implicit location of this voice.

Balthasar is fundamentally, I have suggested, an *unfettered* theologian, and this is both his strength and his weakness. If one considers his biography, one finds a man of enormous intellectual capacity and creativity who is in some sense, philosophically and theologically, an

---

1. *Twentieth-Century Catholic Theologians* (Oxford: Blackwell, 2007), p. 144.

autodidact, who never holds an academic position, who leaves behind the constraints of an established religious order, who suffers ecclesiastical marginalization because of his association with a most unusual mystic, who becomes his own publisher. All this, I am suggesting, contributes to the creativity and originality of his work. All this means that he is able to open up new and fruitful avenues for theological reflection; rather than struggling to modify existing theological paradigms in one respect or another, he is able to devote his quite intense intellectual energies to developing a very new kind of synthesis. But all this also means that there is an absence of a sense of restraint, of a sense of theological limit, of something like theological responsibility, in Balthasar's work. He had neither the education, nor the students, nor the colleagues, nor the editors, to hold him to account, to restrict or question him, even to make him conscious of himself as one voice among others.

An examination of some of the central images and patterns of thought which structure Balthasar's theology has on the one hand provided a way to gain some sense of the distinctive style and approach of his work, and its impressive sweep, and on the other hand has allowed us to formulate questions about its implicit presuppositions. At the very least, an examination of these images and patterns of thought reveals the extraordinary intellectual ambition of the project, presupposing again and again the possibility of surveying and synthesizing — or surveying and coordinating — enormous swaths of thought, of culture, of tradition; but I have argued beyond this that in some cases to probe the way Balthasar uses these images is to find him engaged, not just in a very big project, but in an impossible one, or at least in one which by his own account *ought* to be impossible. It is to find him writing from a position outside a drama to which there is, on his own account, no outside; to find him writing from a position of a grasp on the transcendent which, by his own account, must escape the grasp of us all.

Treatments of the Trinity and gender were intended on the one hand to familarize readers with two of the most striking and widely discussed aspects of Balthasar's thought, and on the other hand to strengthen, by case study as it were, the thesis that Balthasar's theology is fundamentally over-reaching, that it silently presumes a position which by its own account ought to be impossible.

But is all this fair? Is it all, perhaps, based on a fundamental misapprehension of what Balthasar is really up to? Is it all somehow getting the wrong end of the stick? In what follows I will consider three possible objections to the "very critical" element of this volume.

"Truth Is Symphonic"

A significant theme in Balthasar's writings is the importance of the whole, of seeing the whole in the part, the part in its relation to the whole. And on Balthasar's reading of the past few centuries, the vision of the whole is something with which modernity in particular has lost touch. Might there not be, it could be asked, underlying the criticisms I have been raising, something very like a modern anxiety towards wholeness, a refusal to countenance even its possibility? Is not my critique of Balthasar, in other words, in fact grist for his mill? Is this not just what one would expect from a thinker caught in the toils of modernity? In finding fault with his work in this way, am I perhaps merely reasserting, unquestioned, precisely that modern narrowness of vision, even blindness, which Balthasar believes must be called in question?[2] One of

---

2. Another formulation of the objection might be that I am somehow taking a Protestant position. In Balthasar's collection of aphorisms, one finds one that directly links being Catholic with having the perspective of the whole: "People find fault with the Catholic's feeling of superiority. But how could the fact that he has been put right in the centre of truth (even if through pure grace) not have an effect, too, on his feelings about life? To be able to judge the parts (the sects, the sector) from the perspective of the whole; to see without being seen; to weigh without being weighed, in the sense of Paul's affirmation: 'The spiritual man judges all things but is himself judged by no one.' Catholic writers have often tried to imitate the anguished 'existentialist' tone of their Protestant counterparts, but that garment does not fit them any better than his father's top hat fit Little Johnny Upstart" (*The Grain of Wheat*, p. 120). So if I raise worries about taking "the perspective of the whole," does this mean I am refusing to think like a Catholic, or refusing to allow Balthasar to do so? My own view is that a Catholic's relation to the whole ought to be more one of desire and openness than one of achieved perspective: I must avoid anything which involves cutting myself off from the whole, without ever supposing I myself to have attained the whole or the perspective of the whole. But in any case, as I try to indicate over the next few paragraphs, the direction of this volume has been to indicate that *even by his own standards* Balthasar, in the way he presupposes a grasp of the whole,

Balthasar's most explicit reflections on the theme of wholeness is offered under the title *Truth Is Symphonic*, and a consideration of this little volume — or at least of its central image — will provide us a context for considering whether my argument is fundamentally question-begging.

"A bass trumpet is not the same as a piccolo; a cello is not a bassoon,"[3] writes Balthasar: in a symphony orchestra we find a way of conceiving of difference without either denigration or conflict. The diverse instruments cannot be reduced to one another or derived from one another. They are different, each good in themselves, and good precisely in their difference; they come together to create something greater than any of them. The symphony as a piece of music, more particularly, is an image of a whole which is not a system. One cannot reduce it to a set of principles, or predict in advance how the music will go, but after the fact its unity and even perhaps a certain necessity is clear. The pluralism — of the instruments, of competing themes within the music itself — is not in conflict with, but is a part of, an expression of, the wholeness of the music. And in Balthasar's hands the image of an orchestra playing a symphony becomes still more intriguing. He likens the musicians tuning up to creation before the incarnation: "each player plays to himself, while the audience take their seats and the conductor has not yet arrived." But it is not sheer cacophony: "someone has struck an A on the piano, and a certain unity of atmosphere is established around it; they are tuning up for some common endeavor. . . . Before the Word of God became man, the world orchestra was 'fiddling' about without any plan: worldviews, religions, different concepts of the state, each one playing to itself. Somehow there is the feeling that this cacophonous jumble is only a 'tuning up': the A can be heard through everything, like a kind of promise."[4]

This is undoubtedly an evocative image, a rich conception of the relation of unity and difference, and indeed of the relation of creation and the pre-Christian to Christ. It is also, it is worth noting, an image capable of bearing a theologically modest interpretation. That is to say, it would be

---

presupposes an impossible knowledge. He is, as I suggested in the introduction, engaged in a performative contradiction.

3. *Truth Is Symphonic: Aspects of Christian Pluralism*, trans. Graham Harrison (San Francisco: Ignatius, 1987), p. 7.

4. Ibid., p. 8.

possible to suppose that truth is symphonic, and yet that this is a symphony that we are able to hear only in snatches. Perhaps for the most part, because we can catch only a bit in the middle, or because we are seated too close to the drums, or because of the simple limitations of our hearing, we cannot entirely make sense of what we hear, can only perceive it as incomplete, unresolved, even at times perhaps discordant. Revelation, one might say, allows us to catch *something* of the music, and to trust that there is indeed a whole symphony, but it does not allow us to *hear* the whole.

Balthasar, however, is not inclined to take the image in such a direction. He tends not only to suppose that theological pluralism is contained within a larger whole, but to expend tremendous efforts to lay this out for his readers to see; not only to suppose that Christ is the fulfillment of all possible philosophies, but to try to show again and again how this is so. His is unquestionably an oeuvre of extraordinary intellectual ambition. But what we have tried most fundamentally to bring out and to subject to questioning in the previous chapters, is not just that his range is wide rather than restricted, his claims broad rather than narrow, but the way repeatedly Balthasar seems to write from a position, with a perspective, which on his own account ought not to be possible. He, or at least his voice, seems to transcend the transcendent, to escape the drama, to speak from within the deliberations of the Trinity. It is not just, then, that Balthasar seems to hope to hear more of the symphony than one with a different theological style might, but that he seems to hear it in ways that would in principle seem impossible to all but God.

Henri de Lubac's eulogy to Balthasar praises the sheer scope of his work by drawing on this same image of a symphony, but interestingly, in a slightly different way:

> If there is a Christian culture, then here it is! Classical antiquity, the great European literatures, the metaphysical tradition, the history of religions, the diverse exploratory adventures of contemporary man and, above all, the sacred sciences, St. Thomas, St. Bonaventure, patrology (all of it) — not to speak just now of the Bible — none of them that is not welcomed and made vital by this great mind. Writers and poets, mystics and philosophers, old and new, Christians of all persuasions — all are called on to make their particular contribution.

All these are necessary *for his final accomplishment,* to a greater glory of God, *the Catholic symphony.*[5]

The allusion to Balthasar's *Truth Is Symphonic* here seems clear — so clear that it might be easy to miss, at first reading, the variation in the way the metaphor works. Balthasar's theology, or more broadly Balthasar's whole writing, editing, and publishing career, is conceived as an act of bringing together the most different of sources into a universal ("Catholic") and beautiful symphony, of taking many and varied pieces both within the tradition and outside it and making something whole. But the one who coordinates, who brings together and accomplishes the symphony, in this version, is not God, but Balthasar.

No reason, of course, that de Lubac should use a metaphor in precisely the way Balthasar does, or that one should hold Balthasar accountable for its use (after his death, indeed) by de Lubac. And yet this directs us nevertheless to what seems to me the vital issue: what I have tried to show in the preceding chapters is that the way Balthasar tells us about the symphony of revelation is a way which would not be possible if it really is *God's* symphony, a way which would only be possible if it is in fact *Balthasar's* symphony.[6]

---

5. Henri de Lubac, S.J., "Witness of Christ in the Church: Hans Urs von Balthasar," in *Hans Urs von Balthasar: His Life and Work,* ed. David L. Schindler (San Francisco: Ignatius, 1991), pp. 272-73, emphasis added in final sentence.

6. Although this conclusion is not derived from Karl Rahner, it turns out to echo a comment he once made in a private meeting. Philip Endean, in an interesting article on the relation of Rahner and Balthasar, cites the following comment from the former, made a year after the publication of *Truth Is Symphonic:* "If we were to behave as if our being Christian gave us a 'world-view' in which everything fits together harmonically, we would, in the end, be setting ourselves up to be God. This is because the whole of reality is a symphony only for him. To make pluralism into a symphony — as good old Balthasar does — a symphony which we can hear as such: this is fundamentally impossible"; this comment, made in a private meeting, was recorded in "Leben in Veränderungen — Perspektiven der Hoffnung für die Gesellschaft Jesu" (Karl-Rahner-Archiv I B 46), cited in Endean, "Von Balthasar, Rahner, and the Commissar," *New Blackfriars* 79 (1998): 35. Endean's own take on the difference between the two positions is uncompromising: "Rahner's epistemology is more, not less, God-centered than von Balthasar's. This God-centeredness leads Rahner into a disciplined tentativeness. The kind of security von Balthasar seeks in Christianity is an idolatrous illusion" (ibid.).

Theology and Spirituality

Balthasar is known for his desire to overcome the divide between theology and spirituality, and for describing his own work as "kneeling theology." A second objection, then, might be that the critique of the previous chapters is based on a failure to appreciate the *genre* of his work, that my criticisms arise from approaching Balthasar as though he were producing standard academic theology, when in fact he is not. If Balthasar's writings arise from, and are meant to lead into, contemplation and reverence, rather than critical analysis and debate, then do my concerns not somehow fundamentally miss the point?

An obvious first step in considering such an objection is to look at Balthasar's own writing on the topic of theology and spirituality, and perhaps the most obvious place to turn for this is an essay in the first volume of *Explorations in Theology* entitled "Theology and Sanctity." The fundamental theme of this piece is of a unity that has been lost: before the scholastics, theology and sanctity, or theology and spirituality, were united; since the scholastics, they have been divided. Balthasar does not simply advocate a return to the way things were in the first millenium,[7] but *some* kind of a retrieval of the unity of these two things is clearly needed.

I have rather loosely, in the previous paragraph, moved between "sanctity" and "spirituality," and in fact this reflects a certain elision in Balthasar's thought. To the question "what is it that ought not be separated from theology?" there are in fact two rather different answers. One can, on the one hand, say that theology and *life* ought not be separated, so that theologians, in their life as a whole, ought to exhibit what they teach in their theology — and Balthasar does indeed say this. Or one can, on the other hand, say that *reflection* on the nature of Christian life, or spirituality, in the sense of spiritual theology, ought not be separated from dogmatic theology — and Balthasar does indeed also say this. In fact he moves from one to the other without seeming to notice that any

---

7. "No one would think of denying that the gain in clarity, insight, and mastery of the entire field [as theology increasingly took on a 'scholastic' form] was enormous" (pp. 184-85); thus he entitles the third section of the essay "Towards a *New* Unity" (emphasis added).

transition has been made. The essay begins very firmly with the question of the relation between theology and the *life* of the theologian: hardly anything in the history of Catholic theology, Balthasar asserts, is "less noticed, yet more deserving of notice" than the fact that before the scholastics the great saints were mostly theologians, and that since the period of high scholasticism "there have been few theologians who were saints."[8] Theologians in the earlier period were "complete personalities . . . [who] lived what they taught with such directness, so naively, we might say, that the subsequent separation of theology and spirituality was quite unknown to them."[9] Balthasar makes, however, a sudden shift of register, to a focus on the written *works* of these figures: in the sentence which immediately follows the one just quoted, Balthasar asserts that "It would not only be idle but contrary to the very conceptions of the Fathers to attempt to divide their works into those dealing with doctrine and those concerned with the Christian life (spirituality)."[10]

This distinction is worth noting, because whereas quite serious difficulties might be raised about the connection Balthasar draws here between being a theologian and being a saint,[11] the notion that dogma and spirituality, theology and an account of the spiritual life, were in fact integrated *in their writings* is relatively uncontroversial. Balthasar is quite right to point to the divide between spiritual theology and dogmatic theology as something peculiarly modern, or at least post-scholastic, and his sense that something is troubling about this divide, that this poses a problem for us, is one widely shared.

What, then, does Balthasar propose should be done about overcoming this divide? The gist of his essay, I think, is not simply to exhort theologians to be more saintly, or to tell those who are eventually to be recog-

---

8. "Theology and Sanctity," p. 179.

9. Ibid., pp. 182-83.

10. Ibid., p. 183.

11. One might want to ask questions, for instance, about factors that have contributed at one period or another to the Church's official recognition of saints; one might want to ask in particular whether some of the great patristic theologians were in fact *anything but* edifying exemplars of the Christian life; one might wonder whether Balthasar's language of the saints living what they taught so "directly" and "naively" is not suggestive of a degree of romanticizing nostalgia.

nized as the saints of our generation to write more theology. He seems to presume now that on the whole saints and theologians will be two separate groups, but his suggestions cluster around the notion that the one group needs to pay more attention to the other: theologians need to learn from the saints. Partly it is a matter of the overall attitude and orientation of the theologian. So, for instance, Balthasar writes that theology must always resist the temptation to abstract from revelation, "to look at historical revelation as a past event, as presupposed, and not as something always happening, to be listened to and obeyed" and then goes on to tell us that "The saints have always been on guard against such an attitude";[12] or again, that the one desire of the saints is "to be receptive, men of prayer" and that this is the "tacit presupposition of any systematic theology."[13] And so, in sum, "Knowledge must never be separated from the attitude of prayer with which it began. . . . There is no such thing as a theological investigation that does not breathe the atmosphere of 'seeking in prayer.'"[14]

But it is not only an attitude that is to be learned from the saints. Particular doctrinal loci, Balthasar also suggests, ought to be thought through afresh in connection with their experience. For the most part what he seems to be suggesting is that, in light of the experience of the saints, we should approach familiar material from a new angle, a fresh perspective,[15] but in some cases Balthasar points to the experience of the saints as something more like a supplementary source of information, as new data. Christ's "inner experiences" in the Passion, for instance, which he suggests "should constitute the center of the doctrine of redemption," are not very thoroughly described by the New Testament,[16] and we need to look elsewhere — to the Old Testament, but

---

12. "Theology and Sanctity," p. 205.

13. Ibid., p. 206.

14. Ibid, p. 207.

15. In relation, for instance, to a whole variety of ecclesiological questions (or, as Balthasar puts it, issues that come under the third article of the creed), "much would appear in a very different light if we were to apply our reflections to the archetypal function of the saints rather than to the figure presented by the average sinner" (p. 200).

16. "The New Testament gives us very little that can serve to introduce us to the mysterious inner world of the Passion" ("Theology and Sanctity," p. 199).

most of all to "the graces of participation in the Passion given to the Church, the experiences of the saints"[17] — to find the material for dogmatic reflection.

What is the implication of all this, then, for the way we should read his theology? The first thing that must be said is that in spite of Balthasar's nostalgia for the "complete personality," for the theologian who is also a saint, there is no real suggestion in the essay that Balthasar would want to point to his own saintliness, to his own sanctity, as in any way a guarantee for his theology. The essay would, however, lead us to expect two things: first, that Balthasar's theology should look to the experience of saints as in some way or another a theological source; second, that we should find in his theology "the attitude of prayer," the "atmosphere of seeking in prayer." Let us consider each of these in turn.

It is clear that Balthasar does indeed make of the saints a theological source. He writes a number of works on saints, and incorporates studies of various saints directly into *The Glory of the Lord.* One can ask, however, about *which* saints he uses in this way: is it a matter of drawing on the experience of the saints of the past, those who have been formally recognized as such by the Church, or of drawing on the experience of saints of one's own generation? The latter is not a possibility Balthasar anywhere explicitly raises in "Theology and Sanctity" (all his examples in this essay are drawn from amongst those who are long dead and canonized), but in light of everything Balthasar says about Adrienne von Speyr, and everything he says about the inseparability of his mission from hers, it is hard to avoid the conclusion that this relationship between theologian and saint he is describing might indeed be intended also to include his relationship to her.

There is more at stake here, it should be said, than that those who are not yet dead are certainly not yet canonized — more at stake, that is to say, than that von Speyr happened to be alive during much of Balthasar's lifetime. Von Speyr was in fact, as we saw in Chapter Two, very closely associated with Balthasar. He received her into the Roman Catholic Church, he became her spiritual director, he lived with her (and her husband), he collaborated with her in founding a secular institute,

17. Ibid.

he took dictation from her, he edited and published her works. One could say, very briefly, that he is the channel through which she is available; we have almost no access to von Speyr except through Balthasar. And we can presume that her understanding and her articulation of her experiences was to some extent at least — perhaps to quite a significant extent — shaped by his intervention.[18]

"Which saints?" is thus an important question. If we take Balthasar to be commending to the attention of theologians the lives and writings of the canonized dead, then we can see him as proposing a certain shift in the way theologians relate to the tradition, but nothing that would in any deep way alter the fundamental *genre* of theology. But if we take the essay to serve (among other things) as a justification for a theological reliance on von Speyr's experiences, then we seem to be confronting something very different. Then Balthasar, it would seem, is proposing to do his theology in part on the basis of information not available to the rest of us, and information whose nature and value we cannot independently judge. In practice this would actually be rather similar to proposing to do theology on the basis of one's own extraordinary experiences.

A small example from the essay itself may illustrate the point here. At certain points Balthasar makes some rather broad and confident assertions about the attitude of "the saints." For instance, after telling us that the relationship between Christ and the Church is "the center of being in the process of self-realization," Balthasar comments: "This is what the saints are fully aware of. They never at any moment leave their center in Christ."[19] Or again, after warning of the danger of abstracting from the event of revelation, Balthasar embarks on quite a lengthy discussion of the dispositions and desires of the saints:

18. Certainly this seems to have been von Speyr's view, as witnessed by some of her comments to Balthasar: "You see, you always give my experiences such a beautiful meaning. *You understand them much better than I do.* Your guidance really does make the experience meaningful and grace-filled" (*Our Task: A Report and a Plan*, trans. John Saward [San Francisco: Ignatius, 1994], p. 83, emphasis added). Or again, "I'm sorry I can't report it better, but even for me it is totally confused, completely off the beaten track, *en dehors de tout chemin tracé.* But I know that you will see the whole thing and help me. How I need your guidance! How can I ever thank you enough?" (ibid.). Balthasar is here quoting from von Speyr's letters to him.

19. "Theology and Sanctity," p. 195.

The saints have always been on guard against such an attitude, and immersed themselves in the actual circumstances of the events of revelation. They desired to be present, when and where each thing happened. With Mary they sit at the feet of Jesus, hearing from his own mouth the words of revelation. They want to know what the Lord says to them, and nothing else. They do not want to stop listening, not for a single moment, to what is being revealed. . . . Their dealings are with God and him exclusively. Everything, even what they know already, they wish to hear from him, as if they had never heard it before. They wish to have the world explained anew, interpreted afresh, in the light of revelation. . . . They are almost fanatically exclusivists, for they see this approach as the surest way to the universality and catholicity of the truth. They are not perturbed about how to reconcile the supernatural and natural orders, faith and reason, the secular and the ecclesiastical spheres, for they know that those whose standpoint is firmly fixed in Christ are relieved of concern for these.[20]

Now, there are two ways in which one might read these comments. Perhaps Balthasar is generalizing and extrapolating from publicly available historical record — starting from what has been written about and by particularly saints and reaching a variety of conclusions. In this case one might feel there is a certain intellectual sloppiness involved. Balthasar makes broad generalizations, offers few examples, and writes with a kind of incautious directness about the dispositions, feelings, and inner attitudes of the saints that one would never find in a historian. But perhaps one should not read them in this way at all. Perhaps Balthasar is *not* beginning from publicly available historical materials. One of the things Balthasar tells us about von Speyr is that she was given "insight into the prayer life of numerous saints."[21] She was able, more particularly, "to put herself in the place of individual saints or other faithful in order to see and describe their prayer, their whole attitude before God, from this interior viewpoint."[22] She was able to do this on Balthasar's own request,

20. "Theology and Sanctity," p. 205.
21. *First Glance at Adrienne von Speyr*, trans. Antje Lawry and Sergia Englund, O.C.D. (San Francisco: Ignatius, 1981), p. 72.
22. Ibid.

even if the saint was in fact unknown to her; portraits of approximately 250 saints emerged in this manner. So perhaps the description that he gives here of the attitude of the saints is not something extrapolated from historical sources at all, but something drawn from von Speyr's direct, firsthand knowledge; perhaps, to put it very briefly, he is relying on knowledge drawn from heaven[23] rather than from history.

The question with which we began this section is whether my critique of Balthasar is somehow based on a misunderstanding of the genre of his work, because it does not take into account how closely theology and sanctity, theology and spirituality, are interwoven. In order to focus the question, we turned to his seminal essay "Theology and Sanctity." What has become clear now is that there is indeed one reading of this essay, and of his work in the light of the essay, which would support such an objection. If we take "Theology and Sanctity" to be an apologia, among other things, for the reliance of Balthasar's work on von Speyr, then perhaps he needs to be read in quite a different way than I have been reading him in the previous chapters. Perhaps, rather than raising questions about how he can know all that he seems to know, about whether his theology is consistently over-reaching in its claims, about whether he assumes an impossible standpoint from which to write, we should instead assume, whenever he seems to know more than we can understand, or to go further than we would imagine possible, or to write from a perspective beyond what seems possible, that it is here precisely that he is relying on the extraordinary gifts and experiences of Adrienne von Speyr. His work, we could say, represents a synthesis of his vast knowledge of the tradition and her extraordinary mystical experiences; where we cannot explain what he says in terms of the former, we must presume it is accounted for by the latter.

However, although such an approach might cut off my own kind of criticism (and many others with it) it would not in my view be a charitable way of reading Balthasar. Von Speyr's experiences were in many respects unusual, and to interpret Balthasar in this way would be to make

---

23. The special nature of Adrienne von Speyr's charism, as both Balthasar and von Speyr herself understood it, was that she was able to live simultaneously in heaven and on earth, or at least to move freely between the two.

the credibility of his theology rest on the authenticity of her experience, which in turn we know almost entirely through him. To put it rather crudely, to read him in this way would be to read him as saying: this is the way things are, and you should believe it because I say so, and I can say so because I know someone who has been to heaven and seen it to be this way. My suggestion, then, is that although Balthasar may be susceptible to such a reading at times, we do not for the most part *have* to read him in this way, and we ought to avoid it if we can.

This does not mean that we cannot allow that von Speyr was important for Balthasar, or that in many ways she may have shaped his theology. But it is necessary to distinguish, I would suggest, the question of what influences or indeed inspires a theologian — a matter of history and biography — from the way they justify their theological positions — a matter of the logic of the theology itself. Von Speyr was clearly important in the development of Balthasar's thought; whether an appeal to her is necessary for the very logic of his thought is a different matter, and one where for the most part there is far more ambiguity. Charitable reading, I am suggesting, means that we should not presume this second kind of dependence where we do not have to.

A final issue to address in the section is the question of an "attitude of prayer" in Balthasar's theology, or an "atmosphere of seeking in prayer." This is something that the "Theology and Sanctity" essay, as well as Balthasar's description of his own as a "kneeling theology," might lead one to look for. Might it be that the critique I have laid out is somehow a critique from the perspective of "theology at the desk," out of place in the context of a kneeling theology?

In my judgment, though there is indeed something distinctive about the atmosphere of Balthasar's theology, it is not in fact so much reminiscent of one who prays as it is of one who directs the prayer of another. It is rare to find in Balthasar anything of the questing, wrestling, dialogical style of the classic works of theology in prayer of an Augustine or Anselm.[24] But one can quite easily hear in his works the overtones of the

---

24. This is not to say one can find no twentieth-century theology which preserves this style. Cf. for instance Karl Rahner's *Encounters with Silence* (South Bend: St. Augustine Press, 1999).

retreat director, speaking intimately, directly, confidently to his audience, working to bring them to the point of breaking down their barriers, of becoming open afresh to the gospel. Leading retreats seems in fact to have been a, if not the, staple activity of Balthasar's priestly ministry, and it is not hard to hear in some at least of his writings an extension of this activity.

The spiritual director has, it should be noticed, a distinct kind of authority. In the context of a retreat, one does not look to the director as one voice among many, someone making more or less contestable intellectual proposals which need to be sifted and judged; one looks to him much more naturally as a source of wisdom, as a guide to be followed. In fact, in the context of a retreat, if one spent one's time weighing and sifting and critically analyzing the director's advice, one would be eliminating the possibility of actually engaging in the retreat. A certain suspension of the argumentative and critical sides of one's intellect, one might say, is a normal aspect of the practice. And this gives the director of the retreat a very peculiar kind of authority.

But of course retreat directors do not usually display the erudition that Balthasar does, nor the intellectual ambition, nor the polemical tendencies. They do not usually invoke the authority of a massive knowledge of traditions of literature, drama, philosophy, and theology. So if one wants to say that we find in Balthasar an unusal blend of theology and spirituality, then what we also must say is that we find in Balthasar the conflation of two distinct kinds of authority — the authority of the spiritual guide and the authority of the scholar. And this, I think, means that it is not less, but all the more necessary, to worry if his theology over-reaches, if he presumes to know more than can be known.

But Don't They All?

A final objection to consider is this: perhaps it is unfair to single Balthasar out for the kind of critique I have been developing, because perhaps this accusation could be made against *any* theologian. If to do theology is, in the classic formulation, to consider "God and all things in relation to God," is there not something intrinsically over-reaching in theology by its very nature? It might seem that the ultimate implication of my critique is that no one should write theology, or that if they do, they should only proceed in the most anemic, cautious, self-doubting way. Is it the case that if we heed my critique of Balthasar we can only accept a certain kind of methodologically restricted liberal theologian who ventures to make claims about human experience, but nothing beyond?

I think the last four chapters should have shown that there is something quite *peculiarly* over-reaching about Balthasar; that his work is routinely prone to silently assuming an extraordinary, and unwarranted, authority; that his is an authorial voice that regularly seems to speak to us from an impossible position. The case that has been built in the last few chapters, in other words, really is about *Balthasar* and not about theology as such. It may of course be true that for any theologian over-reaching remains a possibility, and a danger. But part of the characteristic depth and seriousness of the major figures of the Christian theological tradition, it seems to me, is the way they provide breaks and safeguards against this very tendency, against the presumption of a God's eye view. This is obviously a very large claim, and it is beyond the scope of the chapter to make the case for it in detail, but we can here at least briefly consider two examples.

Thomas Aquinas's *Summa theologiae* — in which the classic formula about "God and all things in relation to God" can be found — is not a work which would normally be characterized as excessively anemic, cautious, or self-doubting. And yet, on a number of grounds, I do not think it could reasonably be accused of presuming a God's eye view.

First of all, though the *Summa* is an extraordinarily ambitious synthesis,[25] it is also shaped by a profound apophaticism. This is not just something that manifests itself in one or two programmatic statements but over and over again. Aquinas's treatment of the nature of religious language is one example. On some readings, at least, his doctrine of analogy is no moderate balancing act — where we can describe God *quite* well, but just not perfectly — but has a distinctly apophatic bent: although we can know that certain words apply to God, we do not in fact know what we *mean* when we say them of God. Or if one looks at

---

25. Though of course unfinished.

Thomas's notion of divine simplicity, one finds that this is not so much a way of describing God, as a way of ruling out the possibility of any description of God we might imagine, since all language of *composition* is rejected. Even if one looks at Thomas on the Trinity, it seems that though he takes considerable pains to clarify the grammar of the doctrine, he does not so much try to show us how to *understand* the Trinity, as to confront us with the fact that we *cannot* understand it.[26]

Thomas's apophaticism, then, profoundly shapes the whole edifice of the *Summa,* and it is one thing which stands as a kind of break against over-reaching, against the presumption of a God's eye view. Still, this is perhaps not an ideal basis on which to contrast him with Balthasar, for two reasons. First, interpretation of Thomas is contested, and so, though there may be quite widespread support for the kind of apophatic reading I sketched in the previous paragraph, it will certainly not be universally accepted. And in any case, I have deliberately avoided taking Balthasar's more methodological and programmatic comments as my focus, and this makes contrast with a Thomistic apophaticism, which we learn of *in part* at least through Thomas's more methodological and programmatic statements, difficult.

Let us instead, then, consider the way Thomas engages with his predecessors. On one level there is similarity here to Balthasar; Thomas is extremely wide-ranging in his sources. One could say that, like Balthasar, Thomas is on a mission to consider all that has gone before him, to produce a symphony, a massive synthesis, in which all voices of Scripture and tradition, of the philosophers and the Fathers, of ancient authorities and recent scholastics, have their proper place. And yet the nature of Thomas's engagement with the tradition — with these voices — is actually very different from that of Balthasar. As Thomas works through his theology, question by question, article by article, indeed objection by objection, he at every stage deals carefully and in detail with the position of others, and article by article, objection by objection, he gives *reasons* for the positions he takes, for the points at which he disagrees or takes a different line from another thinker, for the points at which he is forced to

26. Cf. my "Aquinas, the Trinity, and the Limits of Understanding," *International Journal of Systematic Theology* 7 (2005): 414-27, for a defense of this claim.

choose, perhaps, one authority over another. So whereas Balthasar's treatment of the position of others is often — not always, certainly, but often — quite sweeping, Thomas's characteristic mode is be precise and focused; and whereas Balthasar tends simply to present us with his judgments, Thomas almost always gives us reasons, grounds for the decisions he takes. All this shows a respect for his predecessors, but just as importantly it means that Thomas is laying himself open for the judgment of his readers. Insofar as we have access to his arguments for taking a particular decision, we are in a position ourselves to form a judgment, to determine whether he persuades or not. Thomas allows himself to be accountable, then, both to his sources and to his readers.

Or again, consider Karl Barth. He is not a theologian one is likely to brand as unduly anemic, cautious, or self-doubting. He is an extraordinarily forceful writer, with a tone that is polemical and self-assured, deliberately propounding a theocentric as against an anthropocentric theology. And yet on two levels there is in place, I would suggest, a break on Barth's theology, so that his authorial voice is never in danger of assuming a divine perspective.

Barth is known for his forceful "No!," for sharp debate and disagreement, for taking decisive stands against predecessors or contemporaries — and it is in this very oppositional nature of his theology, I would suggest, that we find a first break against the presumption of a God's eye view. Barth very clearly understands himself as *one* Christian voice in disagreement with others: he stands *opposed to*, rather than above, other theological positions. And if in the twentieth century he thinks it is necessary to make a sharp correction to Schleiermacher and all that followed in the nineteenth century, then he surely expects something new to come along in due course and in some way or other to say its "No" to him. Barth, then, does not operate by surveying all the attitudes or options that are in principle possible in theology, but enters the fray as holding one theological vision in distinction from others, and indeed as inhabiting one theological *moment* following upon and reacting to others. He does, of course, think he is *right* where Schleiermacher or Brunner were wrong, but fundamentally in entering a debate with them he places himself on the same level.

A second thing to notice in Barth's case is that hand in hand with the boldness of his theology comes an untroubled acceptance of that which is not resolved, of questions which cannot be answered. Consider, for instance, Barth's approach to the Trinity. Commentators usually draw attention to the fact that he reintroduces this into the center of Christian theology, insisting with a certain bravado on introducing the Trinity in the prolegomenon rather than (in the manner of Schleiermacher) relegating it to the appendix. But what should also be noted is the way that Barth suggests that the doctrine eludes our understanding, that we have not even the beginning of an answer to the most basic questions it raises. Thus, after having made a case for a change in the traditional terminology — suggesting that we speak of three modes of being *(Seinsweisen)* rather than three persons — Barth points to a whole series of questions with which his new terminology nevertheless gives us no help whatsoever:

> The great central difficulties which have always beset the doctrine of the Trinity at this point apply to us too. We, too, are unable to say how an essence can produce itself and then be in a twofold way its own product. We, too, are unable to say how an essence's relation of origin can also be the essence itself and indeed how three such relations can be the essence and yet not be the same as each other but indissolubly distinct from one another. We, too, are unable to say how an essence's relation of origin can also be its permanent mode of being and, moreover, how the same essence, standing in two different and opposed relations of origin, can subsist simultaneously and with equal truth and reality in the two different corresponding modes of being. We, too, are unable to say how in this case 3 can really be 1 and 1 can really be 3.[27]

Take what care we might, Barth is suggesting, in our terminology, in escaping certain dangers and misconceptions, we still find ourselves up against a series of absolutely central questions which are simply unanswerable. Or again, we might consider Barth's treatment of evil, which he formulates in terms of *das Nichtige.* How can we understand this evil in relation to God's sovereignty? We would go wrong, Barth says, if we sup-

27. *Church Dogmatics* 1.1 (Edinburgh: T&T Clark, 1956), p. 367.

posed that God *causes* evil: "We stray on the one side if we argue that this element of nothing derives from the positive will and work of God as if it too were a creature, and that the Creator Himself and His lordship are responsible for its nothingness." But equally we would go wrong if we supposed that God merely *permits* evil: "we go astray on the other side if we maintain that it derives solely from the activity of the creature, in relation to which the lordship of God can only be a passive permission and observation."[28] Barth, however, does not present a third course which finds a path between these two possibilities. Instead he cuts off all possible solutions: we go wrong too if we think we can find "some central position of neutrality" or can "overcome the contrast between God's holiness and His omnipotence by mediation."[29] Rather than present any resolution, Barth concludes that "we have here an extraordinarily clear demonstration of the necessary brokenness of all theological thought and utterance." We must acknowledge that "our knowledge is piece-work." Theology concerns itself with "the history of the Creator's dealings with His creature"[30] and it must not "be intent on unifications or mediation which are not to be found in the history." However confident and assertive Barth's theology is, then, it is also marked by a genuine willingness to acknowledge limits to what we can know, points at which we lack answers or indeed any insight, points which are unresolved and must simply be allowed to be so.

Now it might be protested that Balthasar's "dramatic" approach to theology is precisely suited for allowing tensions to exist unresolved, for resisting the need for system building, the need, to use Barth's words, for "a complete and compact sequence of thoughts and statements yielded by a principle."[31] As we have already suggested, however, it is not clear in practice that Balthasar's theology really is cast in a dramatic mode. So where Barth's theology simply acknowledges a whole series of questions about the Trinity that cannot be answered, Balthasar's strains, as we have seen in Chapter Five, to give us an actual description of the character of experience of the Persons of the Trinity in eternity. And where

28. *Church Dogmatics* 3.3 (Edinburgh: T&T Clark, 1958), p. 292.
29. Ibid., p. 293.
30. Ibid., p. 295.
31. Ibid.

Barth leaves us with issues surrounding the relation of evil to the sovereignty of God utterly unresolved, Balthasar move us towards a higher perspective where resolution begins to seem possible: sin and suffering find a place, and can be made sense of, in the context of the eternal distance between Father and Son.

* * *

Hans Urs von Balthasar's theology has over the past few decades attracted a great deal of scholarly attention, and he has come more and more to be presented as a major theological guide for our time. If the argument of this book is correct, then one must conclude, first, that the attention he has been given has indeed been justified, but second, that the notion that he might be a great guide, something like a Church Father for our age, has not.

The scholarly interest that Balthasar's writings have provoked is amply justified by the rich creativity of his thought. His writings break in many ways with our familiar theological categories; often he points towards fascinating new possibilities. We have not come to the end of exploring what his work makes possible, of receiving what he has to give, of thinking through where the lines of thought he begins should lead. Attention to Balthasar needs to continue. But, if I am right, it should be combined with a certain wariness, a readiness to question him, to wonder how he knows what he seems to know, to ask where he stands so that he can tell us what he wants to tells us.

A recurring theme in Balthasar's work, as we have seen, is the relation of the whole to the part, the whole to the fragment. In essence what I am proposing in this book is that Balthasar in fragments is important and worth pursuing, for there is much to learn from, to borrow, to think about, to develop. But when one tries to follow Balthasar as a whole, to treat him as one's theological guide, as a contemporary Church Father, then he in fact becomes dangerous. If there is much to learn from Balthasar, the one thing in my view one ought *not* to learn from him is how to be a theologian.

Bibliography

Balthasar, Hans Urs von. *Convergences: To the Source of Christian Mystery.* Translated by E. A. Nelson. San Francisco: Ignatius, 1983 [1969].

———. *Credo: Meditations on the Apostles' Creed.* Translated by David Kipp. San Francisco: Ignatius, 1990 [1989].

———. *Dare We Hope "That All Men Be Saved"? With a Short Discourse on Hell.* Translated by David Kipp and Lathar Krauth. San Francisco: Ignatius, 1988 [1986].

———. *Elucidations.* Translated by John Riches. San Francisco: Ignatius, 1998 [1971].

———. *Explorations in Theology.* Volume 1: *The Word Made Flesh.* Translated by A. V. Littledale, with Alexander Dru. San Francisco: Ignatius, 1989 [1960].

———. *Explorations in Theology.* Volume 2: *Spouse of the Word.* Translated by A. V. Littledale, with Alexander Dru. San Francisco: Ignatius, 1991 [1961].

———. *First Glance at Adrienne von Speyr.* Translated by Antje Lawry and Sergia Englund, O.C.D. San Francisco: Ignatius, 1981 [1968].

———. *The Glory of the Lord: A Theological Aesthetics*

Volume 1: *Seeing the Form.* Translated by Erasmo Leiva-Merikakis. Edited by John Riches. Edinburgh: T&T Clark, 1982 [1961].

Volume 2: *Studies in Theological Styles: Clerical Styles.* Translated by Andrew Louth, Francis McDonagh, and Brian McNeil, C.R.V. Edited by John Riches. San Francisco: Ignatius, 1984 [1962].

Volume 3: *Studies in Theological Styles: Lay Styles.* Translated by Andrew Louth, John Saward, Martin Simon, and Rowan Williams. Edited by John Riches. San Francisco: Ignatius, 1986 [1962].

Volume 4: *The Realm of Metaphysics in Antiquity.* Translated by Brian McNeil, C.R.V., Andrew Louth, John Saward, Rowan Williams, and Oliver Davies. Edited by John Riches. San Francisco: Ignatius, 1989 [1967].

Volume 5: *The Realm of Metaphysics in the Modern Age.* Translated by Oliver Davies, Andrew Louth, Brian McNeil, C.R.V., John Saward, and Rowan Williams. Edited by Brian McNeil, C.R.V., and John Riches. San Francisco: Ignatius, 1991 [1965].

Volume 6: *Theology: The Old Covenant.* Translated by Brian McNeil, C.R.V., and Erasmo Leiva-Merikakis. Edited by John Riches. San Francisco: Ignatius, 1991 [1965].

Volume 7: *Theology: The New Covenant.* Translated by Brian McNeil, C.R.V. Edited by John Riches. San Francisco: Ignatius, 2003 [1969].

———. *The Grain of Wheat: Aphorisms.* Translated by Erasmo Leiva-Merikakis. San Francisco: Ignatius, 1995 [1953].

———. *Heart of the World.* Translated by Erasmo S. Leiva. San Francisco: Ignatius, 1979 [1954].

———. *Love Alone: The Way of Revelation.* Translated by Alexander Dru. London: Sheed and Ward, 1968 [1963].

———. *The Moment of Christian Witness.* Translated by Richard Beckley. San Francisco: Ignatius, 1994 [1966, 1987].

———. *"Mysterium Paschale": The Mystery of Easter.* Translated by Aidan Nichols, O.P. San Francisco: Ignatius, 1990 [1970].

———. *My Work: In Retrospect.* Translated by various hands. San Francisco: Ignatius, 1993 [1990].

———. *New Elucidations.* Translated by Sister Mary Theresilde Skerry. San Francisco: Ignatius, 1986 [1979].

———. *The Office of Peter and the Structure of the Church.* Translated by Andrée Emery. San Francisco: Ignatius 1986 [1974].

———. *Our Task: A Report and a Plan.* Translated by John Saward. San Francisco: Ignatius, 1994 [1984].

———. *Theo-Drama: Theological Dramatic Theory*

Volume 1: *Prolegomena.* Translated by Graham Harrison. San Francisco: Ignatius, 1988 [1983].

Volume 2: *The Dramatis Personae: Man in God.* Translated by Graham Harrison. San Francisco: Ignatius, 1990 [1976].

Volume 3: *The Dramatis Personae: Persons in Christ.* Translated by Graham Harrison. San Francisco: Ignatius, 1992 [1978].

Volume 4: *The Action.* Translated by Graham Harrison. San Francisco: Ignatius, 1994 [1980].

Volume 5: *The Last Act.* Translated by Graham Harrison. San Francisco: Ignatius, 1998 [1983].

———. *Theo-Logic: Theological Logical Theory*

Volume 1: *Truth of the World.* Translated by Adrian J. Walker. San Francisco: Ignatius, 2000 [1985].

Volume 2: *Truth of God.* Translated by Adrian J. Walker. San Francisco: Ignatius, 2004 [1985].

Volume 3: *The Spirit of Truth.* Translated by Adrian J. Walker. San Francisco: Ignatius, 2005 [1985].

Epilogue. Translated by Edward T. Oakes, S.J. San Francisco: Ignatius, 2004 [1987].

————. *A Short Primer for Unsettled Laymen.* Translated by Mary Theresilde Skerry. San Francisco: Ignatius, 1985.

————. *The Theology of Karl Barth.* Translated by Edward T. Oakes, S.J. San Francisco: Ignatius, 1992 [1951].

————. *Truth Is Symphonic: Aspects of Christian Pluralism.* Translated by Graham Harrison. San Francisco: Ignatius, 1987 [1972].

Barth, Karl. *Church Dogmatics.* Volume 1.1: *The Doctrine of the Word of God.* Translated by G. W. Bromiley. Edinburgh: T&T Clark, 1956.

————. *Church Dogmatics.* Volume 3.3: *The Doctrine of Creation.* Translated by G. W. Bromiley. Edinburgh: T&T Clark, 1958.

Beattie, Tina. *New Catholic Feminism: Theology and Theory.* London and New York: Routledge, 2006.

Boyle, Nicholas. "'Art,' Literature, Theology: Learning from Germany." In *Higher Learning and Catholic Traditions,* edited by Robert E. Sullivan. Notre Dame: University of Notre Dame Press, 2001.

Crammer, Corinne. "One Sex or Two? Balthasar's Theology of the Sexes." In *The Cambridge Companion to Hans Urs von Balthasar,* edited by Edward T. Oakes, S.J., and David Moss. Cambridge: Cambridge University Press, 2004. Pp. 93-112.

Daley, Brian. "Balthasar's Reading of the Church Fathers." In *The Cambridge Companion to Hans Urs von Balthasar,* edited by Edward T. Oakes, S.J., and David Moss. Cambridge: Cambridge University Press, 2004. Pp. 187-205.

de Lubac, Henri, S.J. "A Witness of Christ in the Church: Hans Urs von Balthasar." In *Hans Urs von Balthasar: His Life and Work,* edited by David L. Schindler. San Francisco: Ignatius, 1991.

Dickens, W. T. *Hans Urs von Balthasar's* Theological Aesthetics: *A Model for Post-Critical Biblical Interpretation.* Notre Dame: University of Notre Dame Press, 2003.

Endean, Philip, S.J. "Von Balthasar, Rahner and the Commissar." *New Blackfriars* 79 (1998): 33-38.

Flynn, Gabriel, and Paul D. Murray, eds. *Ressourcement: A Movement for Renewal in Twentieth-Century Catholic Theology.* Oxford: Oxford University Press, 2012.

Henrici, Peter, S.J. "Hans Urs von Balthasar: A Sketch of His Life." In *Hans Urs von Balthasar: His Life and Work,* edited by David L. Schindler. San Francisco: Ignatius, 1991.

————. "Hans Urs von Balthasar: His Cultural and Theological Education." In *The*

Beauty of Christ, edited by Bede McGregor, O.P., and Thomas Norris. Edinburgh: T&T Clark, 1994.

Howsare, Rodney. *Balthasar: A Guide for the Perplexed.* London and New York: T&T Clark, 2009.

Jones, Serene. *Feminist Theory and Christian Theology.* Minneapolis: Fortress, 2000.

Kerr, Fergus, O.P. "Balthasar and Metaphysics." In *The Cambridge Companion to Hans Urs von Balthasar,* edited by Edward T. Oakes, S.J., and David Moss. Cambridge: Cambridge University Press, 2004. Pp. 224-39.

―――. "Foreword: Assessing 'This Giddy Synthesis.'" In Lucy Gardner, David Moss, Ben Quash, and Graham Ward, *Balthasar at the End of Modernity.* Edinburgh: T&T Clark, 1999.

―――. *Twentieth-Century Catholic Theologians.* Oxford: Blackwell, 2007.

Kilby, Karen. "Aquinas, the Trinity, and the Limits of Understanding." *International Journal of Systematic Theology* 7 (2005): 414-27.

―――. *Karl Rahner: Theology and Philosophy.* London: Routledge, 2004.

―――. "Perichoresis and Projection: Problems with Social Doctrines of the Trinity." *New Blackfriars* 81 (2000): 435-43.

Louth, Andrew. "The Place of *Heart of the World* in the Theology of Hans Urs von Balthasar." In *The Analogy of Beauty: The Theology of Hans Urs von Balthasar,* edited by John Riches. Edinburgh: T&T Clark, 1986.

MacKinnon, Donald. "Some Reflections on Hans Urs von Balthasar's Christology with Special Reference to Theodramatik II/2 and III." In *The Analogy of Beauty: The Theology of Hans Urs von Balthasar,* edited by John Riches. Edinburgh: T&T Clark, 1986.

McCormack, Bruce. *Karl Barth's Critically Realistic Dialectical Theology: Its Genesis and Development 1909-1986.* Oxford: Clarendon, 1997.

Messmore, Ryan. "Rethinking the Appeal to Perichoresis in Contemporary Trinitarian Political Theology." Unpublished D.Phil. thesis, Oxford University, 2010.

Milbank, John. *The Suspended Middle: Henri de Lubac and the Debate Concerning the Supernatural.* Grand Rapids: Eerdmans, 2005.

Mongrain, Kevin. *The Systematic Thought of Hans Urs von Balthasar: An Irenaean Retrieval.* New York: Crossroad, 2002.

Nichols, Aidan. *Divine Fruitfulness: A Guide Through Balthasar's Theology Beyond the Trilogy.* Edinburgh: T&T Clark, 2007.

―――. *No Bloodless Myth: A Guide Through Balthasar's Dramatics.* Edinburgh: T&T Clark, 1999.

―――. *Say It Is Pentecost: A Guide Through Balthasar's Logic.* Edinburgh: T&T Clark, 2001.

―――. *Scattering the Seed: A Guide Through Balthasar's Early Writings on Philosophy and the Arts.* New York and London: T&T Clark, 2006.

————. *The Word Has Been Abroad: A Guide Through Balthasar's Aesthetics.* Edinburgh: T&T Clark, 1998.

Oakes, Edward T., S.J. *Pattern of Redemption: The Theology of Hans Urs von Balthasar.* New York: Continuum, 2002.

Oakes, Edward T., S.J., and David Moss, eds. *Cambridge Companion to Hans Urs von Balthasar.* Cambridge: Cambridge University Press, 2004.

O'Donaghue, Noel. "A Theology of Beauty." In *The Analogy of Beauty: The Theology of Hans Urs von Balthasar,* edited by John Riches. Edinburgh: T&T Clark, 1986.

O'Donnell, John, S.J. *Hans Urs von Balthasar.* Outstanding Christian Thinkers Series. London and New York: Continuum, 1991.

O'Hanlon, Gerard, S.J. *The Immutability of God in the Theology of Hans Urs von Balthasar.* Cambridge: Cambridge University Press, 1990.

Peterson, Paul Silas. "Anti-Modernism and Anti-Semitism in Hans Urs von Balthasar's *Apokalypse der deutschen Seele.*" *Neue Zeitschrift für Systematische Theologie und Religionsphilosophie* 52.3 (2010): 302-18.

Pitstick, Alyssa. *Light in Darkness: Hans Urs von Balthasar and the Catholic Doctrine of Christ's Descent into Hell.* Grand Rapids: Eerdmans, 2007.

Pitstick, Alyssa, and Edward T. Oakes, S.J. "Balthasar, Hell, and Heresy: An Exchange." *First Things* (December 2006).

Quash, Ben. *Theology and the Drama of History.* Cambridge: Cambridge University Press, 2005.

Rahner, Karl. *Encounters with Silence.* Translated by James M. Demske. South Bend: St. Augustine Press, 1999.

————. "The Layman and the Religious Life: On the Theology of the Secular Institutes." In *Mission and Grace: Essays in Pastoral Theology,* Volume 2. Translated by Cecily Hastings. London and New York: Sheed and Ward, 1964.

Ratzinger, Joseph Cardinal. "Homily at the Funeral Liturgy of Hans Urs von Balthasar." In *Hans Urs von Balthasar: His Life and Work,* edited by David L. Schindler. San Francisco: Ignatius, 1991.

Riches, John. *The Analogy of Beauty: The Theology of Hans Urs von Balthasar.* Edinburgh: T&T Clark, 1986.

————. "Von Balthasar as Biblical Theologian and Exegete." *New Blackfriars* 79 (1998): 38-45.

Roten, Johann, S.M. "The Two Halves of the Moon: Marian Anthropological Dimensions in the Common Mission of Adrienne von Speyr and Hans Urs von Balthasar." In *Hans Urs von Balthasar: His Life and Work,* edited by David L. Schindler. San Francisco: Ignatius, 1991.

Schindler, David L., ed. *Hans Urs von Balthasar: His Life and Work.* San Francisco: Ignatius, 1991.

————, ed. *Love Alone Is Credible: Hans Urs von Balthasar as Interpreter of the Catholic Tradition.* Grand Rapids: Eerdmans, 2008.

Scola, Angelo. *The Nuptial Mystery.* Grand Rapids: Eerdmans, 2005.

Servais, Jacques. "Balthasar as Interpreter of the Catholic Tradition." In *Love Alone Is Credible: Hans Urs von Balthasar as Interpreter of the Catholic Tradition,* edited by David L. Schindler. Grand Rapids: Eerdmans, 2008.

Soskice, Janet. *The Kindness of God.* Oxford: Oxford University Press, 1998.

Tanner, Kathryn. *God and Creation in Christian Theology: Tyranny or Empowerment?* Oxford: Basil Blackwell, 1988.

Trible, Phyllis. "Eve and Adam: Genesis 2–3 Reread." *Andover Newton Quarterly* 13 (1973): 77-81.

Wigley, Stephen. *Balthasar's Trilogy.* New York and London: T&T Clark, 2010.

———. *Karl Barth and Hans Urs von Balthasar: A Critical Engagement.* London and New York: T&T Clark, 2007.

Williams, Rowan. "Balthasar on the Trinity." In *The Cambridge Companion to Hans Urs von Balthasar,* edited by Edward T. Oakes, S.J., and David Moss. Cambridge: Cambridge University Press, 2004.

Index